INHERITING THE JAPANESE WAY

INHERITING THE
JAPANESE WAY
WHO GETS WHAT AND WHY

Wm. Penn

Forest River Press

Inheriting the Japanese Way: Who Gets What and Why
Published by Forest River Press
www.forestriverpress.com
Cover Design: Julie Morikawa

ISBN 978-4-902422-04-7
First Print Edition

This book is a work of fiction. All the characters are fictional.

Earlier versions of six of these stories appeared in ebook form in the now unavailable *Willful Mysteries Series*
(Book One: Who Gets What? Inheritance Stories from Japan, Book Two: The Strange Life of Mrs. Kato).

TABLE OF CONTENTS

PREFACE

WELCOME TO THE world of the Japanese inheritance system—where what you see is not always what you get, and where there is a Will, there may not always be a way. The idea for these stories emerged while researching the risks and complex rules of Japan's distinctive inheritance system for *The Expat's Guide to Growing Old in Japan*. That book is a practical guide to pensions, wills, inheritance, senior housing and health care for expats considering whether to spend their retirement years in Japan, and it is straightforward, fact-filled nonfiction. I hope you will find these fictional stories an easy and entertaining way to understand the intriguing inner workings of the real-life Japanese inheritance system.

*   *   *

PLEASE NOTE EARLIER versions of six of these stories have appeared in ebook form only in the now unavailable *Willful Mysteries Series* (Book One: *Who Gets What? Inheritance Stories from Japan*, Book Two: *The Strange Life of Mrs. Kato*). Now available for the first time in paperback, this new compilation contains recently revised versions of six of those earlier stories and one new story.

MARIKO

MARIKO SATO HAD been blessed with a very fortunate marriage. Her husband was the scion of a very old and wealthy family. He had done his part to increase their riches, and she had lived in luxury all her married life. Sato was the most common surname in all of Japan, and Mariko relished the privacy and anonymity the name gave her. She had never had to deal with celebrity. Her comings and goings and fashion were of interest only to her small circle of equally rich women friends who met often for relaxing luncheons at Tokyo's most exclusive restaurants.

In fact, Mariko had been dining with her best friends Yoko and Reiko when she got the call that Taro, her husband of 25 years, had suddenly died of a heart attack on the golf course. *Pin pin korori* (healthy till you drop over dead), they called it in Japanese. It was the kind of rare, blissfully quick and peaceful departure that had not required the deceased or his family to suffer through a long and painful decline. She did not have to spend years devoting herself to the care of her husband. Yes, her friends agreed, even in this she had been lucky.

Mariko had enjoyed a very good life which was why her friends were shocked to learn of the unfortunate situation she now faced. Most of her women friends had been in attendance at the memorial service held 10 days after her husband's death. People, especially in the circles she moved in, were far too busy to attend sudden funerals anymore. Thus, families were now free to bury their loved ones privately and quietly and face the world later at a memorial service. These were held at a public hall or hotel where a large photo of the deceased, surrounded by floral tributes, loomed over the proceedings. It was a calm, sophisticated approach that took the reality away from death and allowed the busy participants to pencil it into their schedules far in advance.

Taro's memorial service had been proceeding smoothly when two younger women, each with a child in tow, took seats very near the front. It did not take long for the attendees to realize their significance. To everyone's great surprise Taro Sato had had two mistresses, and each had borne him a son. It was not so much the facts of the situation that left Mariko's friends aghast. After all, it was well known that men dallied, especially rich men whose finances were not managed scrupulously by their wives.

Among the women in Mariko's circle, such dalliances were seldom even considered a sensible reason to disturb their comfortable lives and seek a divorce. Although the number of children was not insignificant, it was not a matter of significant embarrassment. Excessive blame or censure was seldom inflicted on men who dallied or their wives who knowingly or unknowingly put up with it. After all, this was Japan. What was really shocking was Mariko Sato's willingness to share the inheritance with these children.

Mariko had no legal reason to be so magnanimous as Taro had not bothered to put the children in his *koseki* family register. This meant that the only way their mothers could prove paternity and the right of their children to inherit would be to petition the court for legal recognition. This procedure, known as *shigo ninchi no uttae,* could be costly and time-consuming and would require the children to take a DNA test. Mariko confided to Yoko and Reiko that she had no desire to force them to do this. She planned to consult the lawyers to see if there might be a way to arrange things so that each of the children would get their share of the estate.

Mariko's graciousness and generosity were so amazing that her friends began to think she was either impossibly naive or going daft. Their concern might not have been so serious a decade or two ago when those then referred to as "illegitimate children" seldom shared in their father's estate. If they were lucky enough to get anything, it was half the share the legal wife's children got. But in 2013, the system was changed. Children born outside the marriage but acknowledged by the father were now on an equal footing. They were at last able to inherit a share of their father's estate equal to what children born inside the marriage would receive.

When first proposed, the law caused quite a lot of discussion and consternation among the public. There were sensible arguments on both sides of the matter. For those who were now enfranchised and able to inherit from the man who had fathered them, there was some satisfaction and justification in at last being able to claim their parent's legacy. Among those born inside the marriage who were considered society's recognized heirs, the view was a bit different. How much was a family supposed to bear? After having to endure the indignity of another woman stealing their husband and father's affections and distressing and embarrassing their lives, they were now told they had to share whatever inheritance there was with the children of the women who had trespassed on their territory. The idea seemed both repulsive and unfair. Like most things in life and in the law, the view was considerably different depending on which side of the fence one was standing on. In either case, it was now the law of the land.

Several weeks after the memorial service, Mariko, slender and sveltely fashionable in a navy blue designer suit and spike heels, was again dining with Yoko and Reiko in a private room at their favorite French restaurant. Mariko had been ravishingly beautiful in her youth and was still stunning at 49. She had a certain presence—poise, tact, elegance and stylish sophistication.

Reiko, the daughter of a wealthy surgeon, shared Mariko's sophisticated charm and style. She was an elegantly dressed women of 50 although her wealth had helped stave off the aging process. Thanks to endless treatments, pampering and a keen fashion sense, she looked not a day over 35.

Yoko was the most laid-back of the three. She was the daughter of a wealthy industrialist and was married to an influential bureaucrat with political ambitions. Her fashion sense was acceptable but not impressive. She looked more her age but had preferred to skip the endless afternoons in the capital's beauty salons and spas to concentrate on her interest in art, music and golf.

"Why worry so much about my skin anyway when I'm out in the sun playing golf two afternoons a week," she always said. She was secure in her status and wealth and less interested in camouflaging her age. Besides, should her husband ever pursue a political career, she thought a more down-to-earth appearance would go over well with middle-aged female constituents.

Both her friends were appalled and alarmed by Mariko's dilemma. All the more so because Mariko did not seem to think of it as a problem herself. Still, they hesitated to be too confrontational. They offered Mariko condolences, commiseration and the names of some very clever lawyers that day, but she had no intention of contacting them and was amazingly calm and placid about her situation. She said she had long known that the other women existed. Taro had supported the children financially during his lifetime. She did not want to be cruel. If the children now wanted their share of the inheritance, she was inclined to give it to them. The women nibbled the delicate appetizers and hesitated to say more until the main course—Kobe steak, so tender it hardly demanded a knife—arrived.

Yoko was perhaps Mariko's closest friend and the one for whom the situation hit home most dearly. Her industrialist father had had his own indiscretions and had married her off to a very powerful, influential and often absent man who she suspected had his too.

"I can't understand your thinking at all Mariko. Why would you not at least fight to get Mia a larger share of her father's estate? I've seen how well you have taken care of Taro all these years and how much he cared for Mia. How could you let these outsiders just come in and take her share away?"

Yoko wondered if there was something more to the story. Were the women blackmailing her? But that did not seem to be the case. Mariko was not at all distraught or pressured. Or was there a skeleton in Mariko's own closet? But Yoko, a fan of the Japanese blood-type fortunetelling method, had done readings on Mariko, Mia and Taro. She knew they were all the reliable, fastidious blood type A, nothing to be skeptical about there.

"I've known about these children for years," Mariko insisted. "I always assumed they would get something. What's the point of taking DNA tests at this point? Why make them go through the paperwork and considerable expense of petitioning the court for *shigo ninchi no uttae*? Besides, Taro was an only child and with him and his parents dead, who would have to take the DNA test on his behalf anyway? It would be Mia, and I don't want to put her through that. Furthermore, all of this would take time and drag the inheritance proceedings out for months. Why bother?"

"It's not right," Reiko agreed. "I should never just let them come in and make a claim without at least proving it finally with a DNA test. They are making you look stupid."

Reiko was not only outraged but a bit suspicious. It was out of character for Mariko to act like this. She remembered 20 years ago when she had first clued her in on the car purchasing techniques doctors used to lower their taxes and how keen she had been to try it herself. Reiko had explained that her father had always purchased an expensive car, a Rolls Royce or Jaguar, and took it off his taxes as a business expense. Then within two years he bought another new car and sold the slightly used one off as a secondhand car saving a considerable amount in taxes in the process. Reiko knew Mariko had been doing this continuously ever since. She was not averse to accumulating wealth, so why just give it away now?

"I don't want to be greedy," Mariko replied. "I will get half the estate and the house until I die if I want it."

Changes to the Japanese Inheritance Law in 2018 decreed that women who had been married 20 years or more were legally allowed to stay in the family home until they died. In Japan, spouses got one half of the deceased's estate and the children shared the other half. In the past, women had often had to sell the family home to raise money to give all the children their fair share of the estate. Or if they were able to keep the house, it often represented the lion's share of their inheritance. They had very little money left with which to maintain it. No, those days were over. The law had finally come to the rescue. Now the family home was the wife's until she died. Then the children would inherit it.

"But it's the principle of the thing that bothers me," said Reiko. "You should at least make them work for it, so to speak."

Yoko concurred and demanded that Mariko wake up and do something. "Isn't Mia mad at you about all this?"

As a dessert platter of delicate pastries, fine chocolates and green tea ice cream in little porcelain cups was put before them, Mariko refused to engage in further debate and her friends tactfully changed the subject. They were determined not to let the unpleasantness put them off their desserts.

Mariko quietly ran her square dessert spoon through the green tea ice cream and carved little hearts in the surface. As her companions, thinking perhaps they had said too much, raved on about the newest designer brand shop in Ginza, Mariko replayed in her mind the conversation she had had with her daughter that morning. It was true. Mia really had not understood, and she was not sure how much of it to explain to her.

Mariko had kept her secrets for a quarter century. What was the point of revealing them now when things were calm? Despite the public perception of her married life, the reality had been somewhat different. They both adored Mia and wanted what was best for her, but they had just gradually fallen out of love with each other. They still kept up appearances though and Taro lavished gifts on her, especially at holidays or when a new mistress was discovered.

Mariko had been very good at getting whatever she wanted. New cars were purchased every two years. She got diamonds and expensive jewelry and designer items for birthdays and holidays. These she had skillfully converted into cash and stocks. She had accrued a lot of her personal fortune by playing the stock market, very skillfully if she did say so herself.

When the first of the mistresses was discovered, Mariko had Taro buy her a holiday getaway home in the Fuji Five Lakes area for compensation. When the second appeared, she had Taro buy Mia a luxury condo in downtown Tokyo. Then Mariko had used some of her personal wealth to secure a condo in the same complex. She rented it out at a considerable profit, but now she thought she might like to live there herself.

Considering Taro was paying for the upkeep of three children, it was clear that his wealth was extreme or at least it seemed so. Part of Taro's disdain for a complex Will was that he was not really sure how much he did have or how long it would last keeping three women and three children in comfortable lives. It sometimes felt like he was maintaining a harem he had no control over. Yet, he was well aware that he could not really rely on any of them to be there for him during a lengthy illness. Indeed, it was fortunate he had died quickly before that reality was more clearly revealed to him.

Still, Mariko had been with him since the beginning; and in the beginning, he had loved her very much. Even in later life, he could not help feeling fondly toward her. Even when he had first learned her secret, he did not dislike her. He just found her a rather unfortunate creature, a cornered cat who had found him a convenient way out of a difficult predicament. He did not reproach her for that.

Mariko had become pregnant shortly before her fiancé died in a car accident. Taro, who had long vied for her affections, quickly figured out her situation. He had not hesitated to offer his help and support and down the wedding aisle they went. When Mia was born seven months later, it was considered a dangerous premature birth. By the laws of nature, of course, it was nothing of the sort; but no one needed to know that but Mariko and Taro. Never once did Mia suspect that the man who was her father, who lavished her with gifts and concern, who listened to all her stories and praised all her accomplishments, was not her real father.

When Mia asked about DNA testing, Mariko had deflected the question. She did not want Mia to realize that she was the one who would not pass such a test. Who wanted the complications of that? Fortunately, Mia was a good kid and did not continue to protest.

"You are right, Mother. We have plenty. We can share. Love is what is really important. Finding true, faithful love and keeping it is my goal."

Despite having been raised with money, Mia was not greedy about the acquisition of more. Mariko relaxed and smiled to herself. She was happy that, for Mia, love was what was really important, and she wondered when her daughter might find that special someone. Little did she know she already had. In fact, that very afternoon Mia was meeting the man she loved and planned to marry.

*   *   *

KENJI WAS WAITING for her in a coffee shop near his small office. He was clever with computers and had established his own startup company right out of college. It was finally taking off, so much so that he had felt confident enough to propose to Mia just a few weeks before her father died. She had accepted his proposal. They had been in love since they met their junior year in college and had never dated anyone else since. They just seemed meant for each other.

Kenji was super empathetic and attuned to her needs. She thought maybe it was because he was the son of a single mother, a mother he had loved dearly. She had died of cancer their senior year. Mia had met his mother several times and helped him nurse her at the end. She seemed happy that her son had found someone who truly loved him and would take care of him after she was gone.

In Japan, it was the custom not to introduce a boyfriend to one's parents until the relationship was quite serious. So Mariko had never met Kenji. Nor had Mia talked to Kenji about her family other than to say her father was a businessman. She hesitated to tell him they were rich. They always met outside or at his apartment, not at her expensive condo. Perhaps, she thought it would scare him away if he knew. But after he proposed, she had told him all about her father's company and her stylish mother. He was a bit surprised but said it didn't change anything. It was her he had fallen in love with way back in college. He was a fiercely independent, self-made man, and he was determined to make it in life on his own. He wanted nothing from her rich relatives. He made that clear.

When her father died a few weeks later, Kenji had been a wonderful support, but she had not yet introduced him to her mother. Mia told Kenji she did not want to shock and further upset her mother just yet. She suggested they wait to tell her until after things had calmed down. Mia was afraid Mariko might be judgmental about his family background and his lack of wealth. Besides, to show respect to her father, Mia wanted to wait at least a year after Taro's death to get married. Kenji understood and, in their own minds, they had tentatively set their wedding date for 14 months later.

*   *   *

MARIKO WAS DETERMINED to give all the heirs their fair share and to only later let them learn how little, in fact, it was. The family wealth was tied up in the company and all sorts of trusts. Although Taro never lacked for anything and spent lavishly as head of the financial empire, his own personal fortune was not huge. Over the years, Mariko had divested him of large sums of it through the expensive gifts that were her due. She had taken them and parlayed them into a not insignificant fortune of her own—stocks, annuities, property (usually vacant lots which were easier to resell), and a few other items too. What the children would receive after all the taxes and expenses were paid would be quite a paltry sum by the standards of Tokyo's super elite. It was indeed good Mia already had her own condo and car and, like her mother, a fashion sense that favored simplicity.

As things turned out, neither Mariko nor the mistresses needed to take any further legal action. A month after Taro's death, the three women met formally for the first time when they were all summoned to the office of Taro's lawyer for the reading of his Will. In the Will, Taro clearly acknowledged that the two young boys were his sons. Acknowledging paternity in this way meant the children were now legally qualified to receive their full share even though they had not been included in the *koseki* family register. Since Japanese law decreed a spouse and children share an inheritance 50-50, this now meant Mariko would get one half of her husband's estate and her daughter, Mia, would share the rest with two half-siblings. Instead of getting 50 percent, Mia would now get a little over 16.5 percent.

Taro also had done everything the lawyers had recommended to make sure the Will dealt with all the corporate matters smoothly, properly and most efficiently, but that was it. He knew his life and financial matters were complex, and he was just as well inclined to let all of the women in his life fight out the details and division of his assets with the lawyers after his death, if they were so inclined. Having always been rich, Taro had not felt compelled to protect that wealth as much as someone who might have worked hard to attain it would have. Besides, he trusted the very clever Mariko would figure something out. She always did.

The lawyer also wanted to know what Mariko wanted to do about the house which was in Taro's name. She said she understood that under the 2018 revision of the Inheritance Law it would be hers until she died if she wanted to continue living there. The lawyer agreed but pointed out some of the lesser known aspects of the new law. If she invoked this clause, it would indeed be hers until she died. However, if she eventually needed to go into a nursing home or assisted care facility, she would at that point most likely want to give the house to the children. That could potentially open them up to a hefty gift tax bill.

Considering the rather complicated family situation and the fact that she had properties of her own, the lawyer suggested one alternative might be simply to include the house in the overall inheritance, sell it now and split the proceeds with the other inheritors. Then she would have only her own personal wealth to manage in future. She discussed the matter with Reiko and Yoko at their next luncheon.

Reiko was shocked. "Give up your glamorous home? Are you crazy?"

Yoko, who was more aware of the ways of the world of the rich and influential, was less surprised. "Yes, if you have to let all these other people share in the inheritance, you might as well get rid of it all at once and be done with them. Holding onto the house only drags out the uncomfortableness for Mia and leaves her to deal with them all again later. Prices are good now. There is no use waiting. Besides, that way they can all help pay for the inheritance tax on the house too," she smiled.

Mariko had not considered that, but it was not a bad idea actually. And if the truth be told, the thought of selling the large home and grounds and releasing the staff who maintained it sounded downright liberating to her. Taro was gone and she was ready to start over.

The lawyers suggested the inheritors all meet the following month to complete the *isan bunkatsu kyogisho,* the official agreement on the division of assets that all inheritors must sign and affix their seals to before an estate can be settled. The lawyers had been with her husband's firm a long time and knew all its inner workings and could quickly ascertain the debts and other matters that needed to be settled. They took care of everything meticulously. No wonder Taro had never much worried about wills and the like. It was one of the great advantages of wealth to not have to worry about all the mundane technical details of life when you had lawyers to do it for you.

When the lawyers revealed the size of the inheritance to the women, it turned out Mariko had been right. Taro had many millions of yen but not billions. All of the children would be very comfortable but not excessively wealthy. The mistresses, who had been steeling themselves for a long and costly court battle, were greatly relieved and agreeable. And so, the day of the signing of the settlement agreement came and went. Well before the ten-month government time limit, the estate was amicably divided and the inheritance taxes paid. Then, the three women who had loved Taro Sato went back to their own lives and never contacted each other again. The only thread that had linked them all was now gone, and they were all free once more.

*   *   *

FOURTEEN MONTHS AFTER Taro's death, Mariko's daughter Mia married Kenji Tanaka in a small, quiet ceremony at a top hotel. Neither the bride nor groom had many relatives. In fact, the groom's parents were both dead.

Yoko and Reiko sat near Mariko offering support and playing the role of aunties. They had known Mia since she was three. Most of the other attendees were the newly-weds' college friends.

"It seems they met their junior year in college, fell in love almost immediately and now—four years later—they are finally marrying. They look so sweet together," Yoko said.

"He's quite handsome," Reiko noted as she stood with Yoko in a far corner of the room observing the crowd. "Something about him reminds me of Taro a bit. They say women often choose men who remind them of their fathers, don't they?"

"Perhaps, but I'd never do that, that's for sure." Yoko had issues with her father, and they were barely on speaking terms. "What does he do?"

"Evidently, he's got his own startup company in the tech sector. It seems to be doing very well, eight employees already."

"Isn't that a bit expensive to set up and maintain just out of college? I hope he is not after Mia's money too."

"Oh, I think not. Mariko said his father had left him some money so he is financially secure."

"That's a relief after how Mia was treated in Taro's inheritance settlement." Yoko had still not forgotten what, in her mind, had been a fiasco.

"Don't raise your voice. You're talking too loud. Someone might hear," Reiko cautioned.

They changed the subject to the fashion choices of the other guests and how beautiful Mia looked in her wedding gown. It was a small private affair so Mia wore just a wedding dress and not an evening gown, colorful kimono, white bridal kimono nor any of the other costume changes most brides endured. Mia's fashion style was very simple yet elegant, always elegant. Mariko wore a lovely peach outfit for the event and made a very stylish mother of the bride.

"Maybe she should start looking for another man now that Taro is gone," Reiko, who was secretly seeing someone herself, suggested.

"Why should she? She has everything. Why complicate her life with another man? No way I would," Yoko concluded.

Mariko looked radiant as she watched her beautiful daughter walk down the aisle on the arm of the man she loved. Later, she couldn't hold back her tears as the young couple left on their honeymoon. At home alone that evening, replaying the wedding in her mind, Mariko felt happy, relieved and a bit self-satisfied too. She had made the right decision a year ago when Taro's estate was settled. It was all behind them now.

*   *   *

MARIKO LOOKED BACK on that autumn afternoon at the lawyer's office as the day everything changed for her and

Mia and Kenji. The mistresses were there too, of course, but they were only peripheral figures. They were agreeable to the estate settlement and had happily signed and affixed their seals to the agreement. The whole thing took no more than 15 minutes. As the other women stepped out the door, the lawyer turned to Mariko and asked that she and Mia stay a little longer. He said Taro had left him instructions that he had to carry out. He ushered them into a more private conference room and closed the door behind them.

Mariko noticed a rather handsome young man sitting in the corner. She was not quite sure why he was there. He wore a simple dark business suit. He was obviously not of the same social class. It was not a stylish designer brand, but he wore it well. She assumed he had some immensely salable skills or talents though for he had a polite, business-like demeanor and an air of confidence about him. He stood and bowed slightly as she entered. As she moved to take a seat, he saw Mia behind her.

Suddenly, Kenji grew quite red and a perplexed look crossed his face. He wondered what Mia was doing there? And what was he doing there for that matter? He had been contacted by the lawyer and asked to come that day in regard to an important legal matter involving his father, but he received no detailed explanation ahead of time.

Before she could wonder what that look was all about, Mariko turned to see Mia's face display a similar expression of shock and incomprehension. The lawyer made the introductions:

"This is Taro's son, Kenji Tanaka. He is the child of an earlier relationship Mr. Sato had before he married you Mrs. Sato. His mother raised him refusing all financial support from Mr. Sato and not even telling Kenji who his father was. She gave him her own surname and listed no father in his *koseki* family register. I'm sorry to have sprung this on you so suddenly and secretly Mr. Tanaka, but I did so on Mr. Sato's instructions. You are no doubt very shocked and surprised to discover all this."

Certainly not more so than me, thought Mia, who was now struck by the terrifying thought that she was madly in love with her own half-brother. No, it couldn't be. It can't be. She wavered and almost fainted. They had to bring her a glass of water to steady her. Kenji too was now looking not red but very, very pale.

The lawyer continued: "Although he was not a part of Mr. Tanaka's life, Mr. Sato has followed his progress closely over the years and wished to leave him something. He has made him the beneficiary of several very large insurance policies."

The lawyer smiled with pride as he turned to Kenji and continued: "Mr. Sato gave meticulous instructions and directed us to calculate the amount of the policies carefully to provide you with as much money as possible while making sure you did not fall into the 45 percent inheritance tax category. And we have done so."

The lawyer then turned his gaze to Mariko and proceeded: "Mr. Sato also made a rather unusual request of me. He left two sealed letters. I am to read the first one to you and your daughter and Mr. Tanaka. I am also pledged to keep the contents secret. Then the children are to leave and I am to present the second letter to you Mrs. Sato and wait in the corner, out of direct view, to witness that you have indeed read the contents. When you are done, you are to burn the letter right here in this room."

A large glass ashtray and a lighter sat on the table. Mariko had already noticed them and thought it odd since there were very few places one could smoke anymore.

He continued: "I am to ascertain that you have indeed done so before I can proceed with the settlement of the Will."

It was all very strange, but they seemed to have no choice. The lawyer unsealed the first letter and began:

My dear Mia, Kenji and Mariko,

If you are all reading this letter now, it means I have passed on, and it is time to reveal a few secrets. First Mia and Kenji, please rest assured you are not brother and sister. You are not related at all. You are free to continue to be in love with each other.

Their startled sighs of relief were drowned out and overpowered by Mariko's gasp of shocked disbelief. Not only was she sitting face-to-face with her daughter's lover and Taro's son, but Taro had known all about it for a very long time. Mariko struggled to remain calm as the lawyer continued reading:

Kenji you are the son I never knew. Your mother would not let me have anything to do with your life and rejected all offers of help and support, but still I watched you grow from a distance. When I realized the woman you had fallen in love with was my own dear Mia, I was both shocked and pleasantly surprised by how fate had brought you two together. I hope that the discovery of my existence will not disrupt your marriage plans.

Mia, you may be shocked to hear this but, although you have been my dearly beloved daughter of the heart, you are not my biological daughter. Your father, your mother's fiancé, died in a car accident shortly after your conception, and I merely stepped in to support her. She will no doubt tell you all about it in time. So, as you can see, there is no impediment to marriage, nothing to keep you and Kenji apart. You have my blessing for a happy life together. Mariko, I hope you will give them your blessing too and support them.

Kenji, you were also called here today by the lawyers to receive the life insurance policies I have taken out and to which you are the beneficiary. I hope they will help you take off in your career and prosper in a way I could never help you while I was alive.

Sincerely,
Taro Sato

The lawyer presented Kenji with the three extremely large policies. He would have no financial worries for a very long time. Then he asked the young lovers to leave the room. Ecstatic and relieved, they were very happy to escape and promised Mariko they would see her at home later.

As the door shut behind them, the lawyer handed Mariko her letter. He took a seat in the far corner of the room to witness that she had indeed silently read it in its entirety. Mariko, still shocked from the revelations about the children, could barely comprehend it all and had no idea what was going on or what she was about to read. Still, she did her utmost to retain her calm demeanor as the lawyer handed her the sealed envelope. She settled herself comfortably in a chair in the opposite corner of the room and opened the letter. It read:

My dear Mariko,

I can imagine you sitting down to read this feeling somewhat relieved that I am now dead and out of your life and that the inheritance procedures are moving along smoothly. Knowing what a tough, fair and clever woman you are, I can imagine you have worked out a suitable arrangement with my other lovers and their children. I can see you being very adult and sophisticated about it all. You always did have great presence of mind and place albeit being a little too trusting of your fellow humans.

Mariko wondered what he meant by that. She had never trusted him around other women. She figured out who the mistresses were very early on and confronted him with them. She did not think she was overly trusting.

I imagine too you are a little surprised to discover the existence of Kenji. I was dating his mother at the time you and Jiro were engaged. She knew I had long fancied you. But since you had chosen Jiro, she and I had become close. She found out she was pregnant shortly after I announced my plans to marry you, and she knew I would not change those plans for her.

When she discovered she was pregnant, she did not want me in her life at all and was very stubborn in not accepting anything from me ever, unlike you who have always taken me for all you could get. I understood that. For you, it was just a marriage of convenience and why not rack up the gifts and perks and leverage them into a fortune of your own. It was a self-defense plan. After all, you never loved me. I never felt you really loved me, and I suppose now we can both admit you never did. No need to keep on with the show for Mia's sake.

Perhaps, Kenji's mother did not want me near him for other reasons too. She knew me much better than you do. She knew what I was capable of, and she did not want her son to be exposed to my ways. I always respected her for that—right up until the day she died of cancer. In fact, she may have been the only woman I have ever respected in my life. But I digress, reflecting on one's life does take one off on tangents, doesn't it?

Anyhow, the main reason for writing this is to let you in on another little secret. It is one that I don't think you ever suspected. This was nice as it always made things rather easy for me. Do you remember back to the day Jiro died? We were all at a resort hotel in the mountains near Izu, eight of us from college, a year after graduation, all spending a week-end together. You were sleeping late. Jiro was driving down to the seaside town for supplies when he lost control of the car on a bend in the road and went over an Izu cliff.

Mariko remembered. She had never been able to for-get that horrible day and the horrible way Jiro had been taken from her at just 24 years of age. And then, there was the even more devastating discovery soon thereafter that she was pregnant with his child. She had very little means to raise the baby on her own. That was when Taro had made his offer of marriage, and it seemed the only way out. One or two of her friends who knew how close she had been to Jiro had thought it strange that she suddenly was marrying Taro, but they were not in Taro's more elite social circle. They quickly moved out of her life as she moved into his world. But why was Taro bringing up all that pain again now?

I'm sure you remember. You were utterly devastated. For a moment, I almost felt a bit guilty but not for long. It was not my fault that Jiro stood in the way of our being together. Something had to be done about that. So before dawn, I snuck out and cut the brakes on his car. On mountain roads like those, I knew it could be deadly, but he was standing in the way of me having you—the girl I had yearned for all through college. So it had to be done, and I did it, and it worked. I had you to myself at last. When I found you were pregnant with his child, I even felt a bit noble about taking on that responsibility, of being your white knight, so to speak. Then, when it became clear you were never really going to love me despite all my kindness, I did not feel guilty at all.

But I suspect Kenji's mother knew something was not quite right with it all. The accident was just too convenient. She knew my potential for jealousy and getting my own way. She was happy to get me out of her life then, but you never suspected.

Of course, why should you? Even the police never suspected. They treated it as the case of a speeding young man, perhaps still a bit hung over after a night of partying. Of course, I gently helped them come to that conclusion. As the son of a rich company president, my word carried some weight even back then. And in those days, there was seldom an autopsy and not much in the way of forensic work on the car. It was really too battered to even bother I suppose. Everyone accepted it as his unhappy fate and indeed it was.

I had, much to my own surprise, committed the perfect murder—one that no one ever found out about. It has always been something of a matter of pride to me, although I had no one to share the knowledge with until now. You might wonder why I did not just carry the secret to my grave with me. But, of course, if there is no one to tell of one's achievements, what good is that?

I felt, as I got older, the need to share my success with someone and who better than you—the woman who has shared my life and fortune. So I got the idea to compose this letter to you and confess all. I don't expect any forgiveness, and I am certainly not looking for any. Rather, I take pleasure in laying it all out to you and leaving you to ponder it and your next move.

Mariko was utterly taken aback. She could not believe what she was reading. He was right. She had never loved him the way she had loved Jiro. Gathering so many nice things around her and amassing a fortune was perhaps a way of compensating herself and covering up the stress she felt in the relationship. But she had never, ever once considered that Taro might have had something to do with Jiro's death.

They had all been at college together, been classmates. She had turned down Taro's advances their sophomore year and had rather prided herself in how they had been able to remain friends despite it. She thought of him as a friend, someone she could trust. That is why she had accepted his offer of marriage. What was he saying now, that it all had been a sham? She couldn't truly process it all. She read through the letter again and again, almost committing it to memory, in an attempt to try to under- stand what was and wasn't real. The letter continued:

> *So now you know my secret, and it is your decision what to do with the information. You could take this letter to the police and have them reopen the case of Jiro's death and spoil my perfect crime and perhaps complicate the estate. That is your prerogative. Or you could just do as I instruct and burn the letter here and now, and no one will ever know. It is up to you. You have always been a smart and clever woman. I'm sure you'll know what to do. Enjoy your life. I did. Farewell, Taro*

Mariko stared at the paper for a very long time. The lawyer was beginning to wonder what was going on, but he waited quietly in his far corner as Mariko contemplated what to do. She did not want to see Taro get away with the murder of the man she loved, but she was also practical.

Jiro, like Taro, had no siblings, and his parents had died long ago. She was the only one who really remembered. His body had been cremated, and the car had been demolished decades ago. There would be no evidence to reopen the case besides this written confession.

If Mariko took the letter to the police and the case was reopened, she could just imagine the sensational banner headlines in Japan's weekly magazines as they went wild over the scandal. She did not want Mia to have to endure that or lose her family's good name in the process? She felt sure Jiro would not want that either. And it would very likely destroy Mia's relationship with Kenji, who seemed a very decent young man far removed from their status-conscious, brand-name world. He would be good for Mia.

Also, if she did take the letter to the police, Kenji and the other children would have to contend with the knowledge their father was a murderer. The resulting publicity and scandal might bankrupt the company. Mariko would also lose face with her friends and social circle although, at this age, that didn't really matter to her. She was astute enough to realize only Reiko and Yoko really cared about her, and even they could sometimes be coy and annoying. Mariko had enjoyed a glamorous, comfortable life, but it did not define her. It was not for herself that she held back but for the children—hers and his.

Bringing Taro to justice would do a great injustice to his family and those they loved. Her lips pursed into a cynical, little half-smile as she leaned back in her chair imagining his smug, cruel, self-satisfaction in passing the knowledge and the burden of the truth on to her. He knew that she knew it was not in anyone's best interests to pursue justice and share the secret with the world. He would thus try to make her his unwilling accomplice in this sick game.

Taro had committed the perfect murder and thrown it in her face with glee, but she would not be consumed by the past or revenge. Rather, she would create the perfect life, exulting in the fact he was no longer in it. He was gone, and she was still standing. She was the real winner. She took the letter and placed it back in the envelope. Then she took the lighter, ignited the corner of the envelope and watched as it burned, flipping it into the ash tray at the very last second. She stared at it until the hot embers cooled to ash. It was over.

"Is there anything else I need to do," she asked the lawyer.

"No, this completes the instructions that your husband left with me. Everything will move along now as agreed to by the inheritors. You should receive the final paperwork in a few weeks."

"Well, that's that then. Thank you for all your assistance."

Mariko appeared composed and serene as she walked out the door and into a waiting taxi that took her to a quiet, secluded hotel pub. Once there, she crumpled into a corner booth and had a strong drink, several in fact. She decided she would never think about Taro or the incident again. Of course, she could not forget it completely. The memory lingered. It returned now and then to haunt her, but she refused to let it consume her. Yes, she was clever, she told herself, and the only way to win was not to be consumed by the pain of the past. That would be her triumph. She would move on and live the life she wanted. And she did.

EPILOGUE

AFTER THE WEDDING, Mariko felt a great burden had been lifted from her shoulders. She took pains to keep up her appearance, but she stopped acquiring wealth. She had enough. She set up a small charity for the children of traffic accident victims from her share of Taro's estate. Some even began to think of her as a philanthropist.

Mariko enjoyed a prosperous, contented life with her friends and grandchildren. She lived with Taro's secret, sharing it with no one, until her own death. Like her husband's, it came on very suddenly one day, 20 years later.

She had just pulled into a spot at the spa parking lot when she was overcome by a massive stroke. She died right there in her sports car. At her memorial service, both Yoko and Reiko agreed that Mariko Sato had been a very fortunate woman.

"She didn't suffer," Reiko said. "That was a blessing."

"Yes, some people are just so lucky," Yoko agreed.

AN ORDINARY LIFE

IF SOMEONE ASKED, he would have to say his was just an ordinary life—nothing exceptional, nothing dramatic.

Makoto Kato worked hard all day. His evenings were spent soaking in a hot bath and enjoying a beer while watching a baseball game on TV. Nothing out of the ordinary, nothing of note, but it was his life. And overall, he thought it had been good to him or at least good enough.

He had never married. He had been in love with his high school girlfriend. They had even talked of marriage until she visited his family home over their meat store in a small shopping district in a Tokyo suburb. When she met his mother, her ardor dissipated. She broke it off and took off. He was hurt but not surprised. He understood that for young women, beginning to test their freedoms in the early 1970s, it seemed far too harsh a life.

After that, his mother set up many *o-miai* arranged marriage meetings for him. Over the years, none of those worked out either. His mother tried so hard to find him a match. It got to the point that every time a woman seemed to be looking at the shop from a distance or passing back and forth in front of the shop, he felt they were observing him. He wondered if they had been made aware of the *o-miai* opportunity and were assessing his marriage potential. Perhaps, he was just being overly sensitive and self-conscious. Maybe they were just looking for the shop with the best prices on pork cutlets.

Several of the *o-miai* meetings had been promising, but they all fizzled out eventually. Perhaps, it was lack of interest on his part, or his mother's reputation for being a very formidable neighborhood fixture, or just the general blandness of the shop. He wasn't sure. Even when a young woman was interested in him, for he was not at all bad looking in his youth, the realization that she would be expected to work with him and his mother in the shop usually made the woman reconsider. He recognized this was not an unnatural emotion.

Why would a young woman marry into all those obligations when she could find a Tokyo office worker with a stable salary who would be gone all day? She would be free to have tea with her friends or relax in front of the TV and watch the afternoon gossip shows. He understood that was a much more attractive life than dealing with demanding customers all day long, slicing meat and weighing it precisely, wrapping it in brown paper and tying it up in little plastic bags. She would have to do it quickly and neatly too as customers easily became impatient if everything was not done with speed and precision. She would have to make change and small talk, clean shelves in the refrigerated glass case in the heat of summer and the cold of winter with drafts coming in through the shop's thin sliding glass doors. There were many worse jobs, but it was not a life a modern young woman would choose if she had options.

Occasionally, a girl was interested, but he wasn't. She would seem too meek or too powerful or not at all his type. Dealing with the neighborhood housewives on a daily basis as he did, he was well aware of what marriage could do to a woman and how it could change her. He had watched many a shy, young bride gradually morph into a determined and formidable bargainer demanding 250 grams of ground meat and not one gram more. His long, real-world experience made him cautious of his choices, maybe too cautious. His mind would hurtle ahead ten years and he would imagine what the young woman before him would look like when she had lost her youth, gained weight and acquired the cheery toughness of a shopkeeper's wife. And then, he could see himself being ordered around by both his wife and his mother or, worse yet, having to intervene in their squabbles.

No, he thought, the status quo was not so bad for him. His one regret was that he had no children, but he also realized he worked so much he might not have been a very good father anyway. He would have had very little time for his children, and they might have resented him for it.

He had fellow small shop owners in the neighborhood association to drink with at night if he wished for company. If he longed for female companionship, he need only travel a few train stops away where no one knew him and visit any one of a number of establishments that eagerly catered to the various needs of lonely men for a price. But, as he grew older, even this didn't really interest him.

He worked hard. He was tired at the end of the day, and there was nothing quite so relaxing as lolling on the *tatami* in front of the TV watching a Yomiuri Giants game and drinking a few beers while nibbling *yakitori* grilled chicken or boiled *edamame* soy beans sprinkled with salt. The Giants were his team. He recognized their problems and their ups and downs, but they were the Tokyo team. They were his team and he followed them loyally for over fifty years from the golden days of Nagashima Shigeo and Sadaharu Oh in the 1960s and 1970s right down to the present day.

The meat shop was hard work, but it was a successful business in the booming 1970s and 1980s when everyone suddenly wanted to eat steak and sukiyaki. The key to the shop's success was his mother's first-rate cooking skills and endless energy. He was proud of her. She had done it all herself.

Makoto never knew his father who was called up in the waning days of WWII and died in the sinking of a Japanese troop ship. His mother, having fled to the countryside with her mother to escape the bombing of Tokyo, gave birth to him in June of 1945. They returned to Tokyo early the next spring where her father had been camped out in a makeshift shack on the spot of bombed-out land where he had happily run the family meat shop before the war. Now everything was lost. Even the nearby temple with the family graves had been bombed out.

Together with her parents, his mother had scraped together a living buying supplies on the black market and then turning them into cheap but filling meals— croquettes, dumpling soup, fried *gyoza* dumplings. Eventually, they were able to build a little shop with a small room behind it for them to live in. Finally, in the early 1960s, shortly before his grandparents died, they had enough money to build a proper, two-story building with living quarters above the shop. By the time he was in his late teens, the shop was thriving, and he was old enough to help manage it. He never thought of further education. He had a business to run.

It was hard work. He was up early every morning to secure and arrange the meat for the shop opening at 10 a.m. Each type of meat was displayed on a large silver or white porcelain tray in the refrigerated glass case. Everything was impeccably bright and clean. The case was polished until it sparkled so that the light shined in on the meat and made it look more attractive.

The uniformly sliced meat was laid out on the trays in layers with precision and artistic flair and covered with a layer of plastic wrap. Little cards describing the cut of meat and price per 100 grams were placed in front of each tray for easy viewing. There was pork—cutlets, thinner slices of fatty and low-fat pork, and small chunks for boiling in stews and curries. There was lamb and chicken and liver.

Ground meat was piled in large, sculpted mounds. Several cuts of beef were available including the paper-thin *shabu shabu*, used for the special hotpot meal of the same name. The meat was sliced so thin it had to be placed on sheets of wax paper and sold that way so that it would not lose its shape before cooking. The trick for getting slices this thin was to use frozen or partially frozen beef in the meat slicer. Makoto prided himself in his ability to slice it so deftly that it virtually slid onto the wax paper.

Everything was done precisely and neatly. One seldom saw a bit of blood on a tray. It was all just about as artistic and pleasant as one could imagine raw meat could be made to look. But at prices of several dollars per hundred grams, seldom were large blocks of meat for roasting on display. And while you could find a few wieners on a tray, the huge, rolled loaves of sandwich meat containing who knows what were absent from Japanese meat stores. Shoppers wanted to know what they were getting. Makoto, who took his job seriously and worked with an almost religious fervor, made sure he always offered the best quality he could get. His customers appreciated this.

Meanwhile, his mother was busy from early morning too. She breaded pork cutlets and took ground meat, mixed it with potatoes and onions and turned it into ready-to-cook croquettes. Years later when busy Japanese women became too harried to fry them up themselves, his mother did the frying too and sold them ready-to-eat. They were a big hit.

If the sliced meat was a day old, his mother preserved it in soy sauce, the sweet rice wine known as *mirin* and a few secret ingredients. Then they sold it for barbecue. She whipped up her own homemade *gyoza* dumplings too which were a great success. These tasks kept her busy all day long. She had just a few hours for a quick rest after lunch before the late afternoon shoppers began arriving.

From the 1950s to the early 1970s, almost every woman was a housewife who stayed home all day. They did their shopping in the late afternoon so they could cook a meal with fresh ingredients each evening for their families and socialize with other neighborhood ladies as they shopped. They, like the shopkeepers, had a strict routine and abided by it. At 7:00 p.m. Makoto and his mother closed up the shop and headed upstairs to prepare their own evening meal.

The shop had done very well. Their location, only a few hundred meters from a small train station, was also good for business especially during the booming 1980s when it seemed everyone had money in their pockets. The Kato family had squirreled away their profits realizing the boom years would eventually come to an end. When the boom years did fade away, Makoto was glad he had not joined in the stock market speculation that other shop-keepers in the neighborhood had tried. He was conservative that way. He preferred to work hard and save rather than invest. You would not know it from looking at him or his slightly shabby shop but, by the late 1990s, he had about 100 million yen, then the equivalent of almost a million dollars, in the bank and a bit more hidden in an upstairs dresser drawer for emergencies.

It was good that he had saved. For as the economic downturn continued, business slowed. And with his mother beginning to show her age, she had cut back on her *gyoza* and croquette production too. The shop was barely turning a profit anymore as women went out to work to help keep their families afloat and no longer had time to cook fresh food everyday. Gradually, the busi-nesses around them that did not have ample savings in the bank began to close. Shopkeepers died, or moved away or absconded in the night fleeing debt collectors. The shopping street lost its vitality. Makoto and his mother were lucky. They still had their savings and could keep the store open for their old customers into the beginning of the twenty-first century.

In 2005, the area was targeted for a redevelopment project, and Makoto was able to sell the land for a reasonable sum. This practically doubled their wealth. He decided to retire and concentrate on helping his aging mother, who he took care of until her death in 2010.

After they sold the store, he wanted to buy her a house, but she wouldn't hear of it. They rented a small, ground floor apartment a few blocks away from where the shop had stood. She wanted to spend her last years in the neighborhood where she had spent her whole life. His mother occasionally chatted with Mrs. Saito, a widow in her late seventies who lived across the way from the apartment, and gave her a dish of her homemade *gyoza*. Fortunately, his mother was not bedridden, just increasingly frail and bent over from all those years of hard work. Her heart weakened and in late 2010, at the age of 91, she passed away.

Later Makoto was glad she had not lived long enough to suffer through the great earthquake of March 2011, an event that shook the whole nation to its core. He made a large, anonymous contribution to a charity set up for the victims of that disaster.

After his mother died, he thought he might take a part-time job in a supermarket meat department just to keep busy, but he quit a few months later. He had been his own boss for far too long. He could not follow the rules of the supermarket trade or take orders from men 20 or 30 years younger and less experienced than himself. Why put up with all of that he thought? Besides, he still had all that money in the bank and not much to spend it on.

He took the sports newspaper and the Yakult lady delivered two tiny bottles of the probiotic yogurt drink to a box outside his door daily. It was not that he really needed either. He felt it was an insurance policy of sorts against dying and being left undiscovered for weeks or months as sometimes happened nowadays in this increasingly impersonal, lonely urban landscape. He also had an agreement with Mrs. Saito across the street. They watched each other's curtains. If they were not opened by 9 a.m., they came across the street to make inquiries. They seldom talked after his mother died, but they were watchful guardians of each other's existence.

The last few years Makoto had been completely on his own with nothing much to do. He'd take a daily walk around the neighborhood and record in his mind how it was changing. There were some streets he barely recognized anymore and fewer and fewer familiar faces. He exchanged pleasantries with the Yakult lady on her rounds. She had a son who must be college age by now. He talked to the newspaper delivery man, who had once in earlier, happier days had his own small shop at the end of the shopping street. They both had been loyal purchasers of his mother's croquettes for many years. But most days, he would just buy himself some food at the big supermarket and wander home without talking to anyone.

His needs were simple. With few expenses and few outside interests, his savings held firm, and he wondered what would happen to the money when he was gone. He had no one to leave it to, no relatives at all. He had started to think more about this lately after he began getting a nagging pain in his chest and shortness of breath. He was 74 now and the long years of hard work (and smoking until he was almost 65) had begun to take their toll.

The doctor said it sounded like angina and gave him some medicine, but he rejected any further medical intervention. Why go through an operation? There was no one counting on him. He preferred to just pass away peacefully or, if not peacefully, at least quickly one day when his heart gave out.

He had already prepaid for his funeral and made arrangements with the local funeral director, who used to be a big fan of his mother's *gyoza*, to have his ashes scattered at sea. That's what his mother had wanted done with her ashes. She said she would be with her late husband that way, but she was also a practical woman.

The family had paid loyally to the Buddhist temple where her parents were buried. When the grounds burned down in a fire, the second loss of a family temple in her lifetime, she consulted with the temple and funeral director and had her parents' remains pulverized and turned to ashes. Then she booked tickets on a boat that took mourners out to sea to scatter the ashes of their loved ones in Tokyo Bay. It was a peaceful moment of farewell, and Makoto had done the same for her when she died. He also knew that she chose this because she did not want to weigh him down with the burden of buying and maintaining yet another family grave for her. And who would be there to take care of it after he was gone anyway? It had been decided the whole family would be buried at sea, and he was at peace with that decision.

There was just one thing that was bothering him. What was he to do with all the money he would no doubt have left when the end came? After watching an afternoon TV program on inheritances one day, Makoto was shocked to discover that if he made no Will, his money would go to the Japanese government. That realization made him determined to make one, but he was still not sure what to do with the money. He would leave the newspaper delivery man and the Yakult lady and Mrs. Saito across the street ten million yen each for their service and concern, but that still left him a huge sum of money to bequeath.

One day when he was feeling a bit energetic, he sat down to type up the list of his assets. Then, he typed up a short Will stating he left his three benefactors ten million yen each and noting the main body of the estate was to be left to two local children's programs. One was a neighborhood daycare where he wished the money to be used for more teachers and better facilities and equipment. The other was an after-school meal program for the growing number of children of struggling, single mothers who needed both hot meals and a place to interact with other kids. He put the Will in a sealed envelope and set it conspicuously in the family's small Buddhist altar to be found upon his death. He felt at peace knowing his money would be used to improve the neighborhood he had lived in all his life.

*   *   *

AND NOW, DEAR readers, you select the ending of your choice.

ENDING NO. 1

WHEN THE CURTAINS did not open at 9 a.m. one morning and the newspaper and Yakult drink still rested outside, Mrs. Saito grew alarmed and called the police. Thus, they found Makoto Kato a mere three hours after his death.

The police found the Will too and turned it over to the proper authorities who read it and frowned. He had typed it all. In Japan, you can only type the list of assets. You have to write out the main body of the Will by hand or it is not considered legally sound. Nor had he dated it. The Will was not valid. With no relatives to lay claim to the money, his fortune reverted to the government. And as far as anyone could tell, it did not go to daycare or after-school meal programs. Perhaps, it went for disaster relief or a new fighter jet, or maybe it paid the salaries of a few third-generation politicians carrying on the family business. Who knows? One can never really tell to what worthwhile or worthless purpose one's tax money is applied.

ENDING NO. 2

THE DATE JULY 10, 2020, was circled on Makoto's calendar. That was the day that the *Homukyoku* (Legal Bureau) would start accepting handmade holographic Wills for storage at their facility, and the charge for this was only a few thousand yen. It was one of the best features of the 2018 revision of the Japanese Inheritance Law.

When a Will was filed with the bureau, their staff would also check to make sure the maker of the will had dated it, stamped it with their official seal and written their name just as it appears on their family register. If every-thing was in order, the Legal Bureau would accept the Will, digitalize it and keep it on file. When informed of the person's death, they would also inform all the inheritors, simplifying things for all those involved.

Thus, for around twenty dollars, people could create a legally sound, registered Will all by themselves. Makoto didn't believe in paying lawyers large sums for things he could do himself. He was eagerly awaiting July 2020. But as his heart got worse, he wondered if he could make it that long.

When the lawmakers passed the revised Inheritance Law in 2018, most of the changes went into effect within a year; but this change would take almost two years to be implemented. He fumed that they were taking their good old time when he didn't have all that much time himself. Then, in the autumn of 2019, he decided he just could not wait any longer. He realized he was watching his beloved Yomiuri Giants win the Central League pennant, for what he knew would be the last time in his lifetime.

He asked the meat shop's old accountant for the name of a trustworthy lawyer. He really didn't trust any lawyers himself but was assured this guy was okay. When he went to see him, he suggested a notary deed will. Makoto showed him his list of assets and last wishes and he prepared the will for him. The lawyer noted it was a good thing Makoto had come to see him because one still has to write the first part of the Will, which declares one's wishes, by hand. Only the list of assets can be typed. If he had died suddenly, his Will would have been void as he had prepared it.

The lawyer also arranged for the two witnesses who would need to be present at the notary public's office and explained how it was standard custom to present each of them with a thank-you envelope of 10,000 yen. This was to compensate them for their time and efforts. Arranging witnesses for a notary deed will was not a simple matter since they could not be relatives or anyone who might benefit from the Will, and they would be asked to affix their official seals to the document. If one was making a secret will, they also were bound by law to keep it secret. The lawyer explained that the notary would charge their fee based on the total value of the estate. Makoto's estate was around 150 million yen, so the price the notary charged would be around 60,000 yen. All told, the Will cost Makoto about 300,000 yen when he could have done it all himself virtually for free after July 10, 2020.

Still, he was glad he had consulted a lawyer. That was always a wise move, he thought, even if one did decide to do it all one's self in the end. Since his health was waning, it was rather simple to let the lawyer arrange everything. The lawyer also provided some good advice on how to minimize inheritance tax liability on his charitable contributions, and the lawyer promised to contact all the beneficiaries after he was gone. Makoto felt he had beat the game and that was a good feeling.

As the cold, damp, wintery air arrived, it all just became too much. Makoto's joints ached and his heart weakened. He could feel it, but what was there to do about it. He was determined not to end up in a hospital hooked up to tubes and wires and who knows what. That was not him. Then late one evening, he felt a severe pain coming on. He took his medicine, but it didn't seem to help much. By early the next morning just as the sun was rising on the horizon, he grasped his chest in one last anguished gasping for air and collapsed on the *tatami*.

When 9 a.m. came and the curtains were not opened, the newspaper was still in the door slot and the Yakult bottles were waiting to be claimed, Mrs. Saito became alarmed. She knocked on his door and called out to him. When there was no answer, she called the police. And thus, they were able to find him a mere three hours after his death. On his refrigerator door, there was a note informing the police of what funeral home to contact should he be found dead and the contact information for his lawyer. And so, the paperwork part of his passing went smoothly.

A few weeks later, Mrs. Saito received a notice from the lawyer to visit his office on a specified date. When she got there, she was surprised to see the newspaper delivery man and the Yakult lady also sitting in the waiting room.

She immediately realized that they must have all been named in Mr. Kato's will.

The lawyer announced that Mr. Kato had no family and thus no legal heirs. So he had specified in his Will that after all the inheritance taxes due the government were paid, they were each to get ten million yen. The rest was bequeathed to two local organizations—a childcare facility to be used for increased staffing and services and a charity that provided meals for impoverished children.

Mrs. Saito noted Mr. Kato had always realized the importance of healthy food. Still, she was cautious. She too had spent her days watching the informative afternoon TV shows, and she knew it was possible for the unsuspecting to inherit debt along with assets. The lawyer assured her that the Kato estate was free of debt.

The three were all quite surprised and overwhelmed by their good fortune. The Yakult lady, who was over 60 herself now, used most of her inheritance to finish paying for her son's college education. She saved the rest to augment her meager pension which she planned to take soon. The newspaper delivery man had some outstanding loans that were troubling him and could now be paid off.

Mrs. Saito had no debts and not much she wanted in life. She decided to save most of hers for future nursing care costs but to also give herself a treat as a way to finally live a little. She contacted her old childhood friend, also a widow now, and invited her on an all-expenses-paid grand *onsen* (hot springs) tour. Except for aches and pains and creaking joints, they were still in relatively good health. They traveled by train from Aomori in the North to Beppu in Kyushu to enjoy the steaming baths. It was the trip of a lifetime for Mrs. Saito and a grand tour that left her feeling quite energetic. She planned to join a neighborhood Nordic walking group when she got home. She hoped to find someone there who might check to see her drapes were opened each morning.

On the fifth night of the tour, Mrs. Saito and her friend sat in a hot springs lounge in *yukata* and slippers chatting about how lucky they were to have had this trip, one of the happiest moments of their lives.

"And it is all thanks to that nice Mr. Kato. It was really kind of him to have remembered you in his will."

"Yes, I never suspected it. What a surprise but a nice one," Mrs. Saito said as she carefully adjusted her *yukata* collar. "And then I thought, what do I want to do with this money? What would bring me the most happiness? And the answer was to have this trip with my oldest, dearest friend and to soak our weary bones and joints in these lovely hot springs."

"Ah, and it does feel good. I feel younger already thanks to Mr. Kato. Do you know I saw on TV that if you don't have heirs or a will, all your money will just go to the government. What a waste that would have been."

"He thought out everything carefully right to the end, and who would have known he had so much money too. It was quite shocking really. And he gave his money to those programs for children. He saw the needs in the neighborhood and tried to help fill them. Yes, who knows what the government might have used the money for if he didn't have a will?"

"Well, you never know. The money might have been put to some good use for disaster relief or social welfare causes."

Mrs. Saito was less optimistic: "or another fighter jet or the salaries of several third-generation politicians carrying on the family business. Who knows what it would have been used for, but Mr. Kato knew what was best. He was an ordinary man with good common sense."

A WALK IN THE PARK

KEIKO THOUGHT HOW nice it would be to just take a walk in the park, oblivious to those around you. How nice it would be to go when and where you want freely. How nice it would be to just walk, think nothing, and enjoy the freedom of it all—finding the first crocus in spring, luxuriating in the fragrance of roses in summer, observing the many shades of hydrangea and watching the pink cosmos flutter in the wind.

Yes, it was a dream, a wonderful dream, but someday, someday she would live it. Reality be damned. Someday she would live it. She thought. She hoped. She prayed, and then she said *shoganai* (it can't be helped) and floated back down to reality.

Keiko was a widow, the wife of the oldest son of a prosperous farming family. Her husband had been good at it and, the weather willing, he turned over a nice profit each year for the family farm with the help of his parents and Keiko. They had raised two daughters together. She remembered once, when they were toddlers, hearing her mother-in-law and her friends chatting over green tea and pickles. They were talking about a young mother a few doors down the road who had been seen taking her children for a walk in the town park in the middle of the day.

"*Mah mah*" they tsked and sighed. "Did she not have anything better to do? No work to do in the middle of the day?"

The message was clear. To spend time with one's children when there was some work that could or should be done was the sign of a very lax young wife. Only occasionally, in the off-season, were she and her husband Ichiro able to escape the constraints of the small town and sneak away with the girls for special family outings of their own.

The older ladies liked to reminisce about the way they were mistreated and forced to work in their youth and how easy the young had it now. They even admitted how easy they themselves had it now with indoor plumbing, running water, modern appliances, comfortable cars and plenty of food, but still the psychological pressures of the past weighed down on everyone.

Keiko felt the story was a clear reminder that one could not do as one likes in a small community. Eyes were always on you. Opinions were always formed and shared. And so, her daughters, like many others, had gone off to live in a city where there was freedom to do as one wants, to walk in the park any old time. Keiko did not begrudge them their freedom. Like most of the women in town, she encouraged her daughters to leave and seek it.

Her husband had two sisters, but they too had got out when they could and only came back now for visits at summer and at New Year's. They came each year laden with rich foods and souvenirs from the city for her in-laws and scant little for her, even though she would be doing the extra cooking, cleaning and serving for their families during their stay. Both sisters-in-law had children who were now grown and on their own. The sisters lived in Tokyo condos far from their own in-laws and had time to themselves to lead their lives as they liked. As she prepared a meal or served tea, she often overheard them talking about their art classes and luncheons and movie outings and overnight trips with their lady friends. It sounded a pleasant life. They never inquired about her life or difficulties.

Still, Keiko knew they would be there in a minute when Ichiro's parents passed on. They would come not just to mourn and help out but to claim their inheritance. In Japan, inheritances went to blood relatives only unless a special will was made to include a daughter-in-law or son-in-law. She knew her in-laws had no will at all and no intention of making one.

Just a year or so ago, the law had been changed so that hardworking, long-suffering daughters-in-law could go to the Family Court and petition the estate of their in-laws for some compensation for their service in the care of the elderly members of the family in their final months or years. However, there was no guarantee they would get anything or how much they would get even if the family did recognize their service.

The government was not exactly overly helpful either. One had only six months to file the claim and the elderly deceased had to have had a *Kaigo* (nursing care) ranking of Level 2 or above. As if just caring for a frail and cantankerous old person was not enough of a chore, they had to be certifiably Level 2.

The caregiver also needed to keep a diary of dates and times and hours although compensation would be calculated at rates far lower than those a home care nurse or housekeeper would get. If the family did not want to offer compensation, it would leave hard feelings all around. To top it all off, even when the inheritors did offer compensation, the daughter-in-law might have to pay up to a 20% tax on the money. It was hardly an enticement to file a claim.

Keiko smiled cynically as she thought about it. What was the point? No, in such cases a stoic approach was better. It would earn the respect of the wider community and the ability to commiserate with others in the same situation. Perhaps, it might even instill a little guilt in the husband's siblings. More than anything, there would be the self-satisfaction of having survived the ordeal. These intangible things were more valuable than a few yen in the long run.

Keiko would have liked to go live with one of her daughters in Tokyo, but both were married now. She didn't want to be in the way, and she could hardly afford to live on her own in costly and overwhelming Tokyo. Besides, she was painfully aware that taking care of the in-laws was considered just how it was in the countryside. A widowed daughter-in-law would take care of her in-laws and the family graves and the home as she always had even though none of it was hers and never would be— and the last thing she wanted was to be in the family grave with them. She shuddered just to think of it. It might have been different if she had a son who could one day take over the farm and take care of her in her old age, but she had daughters.

When her husband died in a tractor accident, the children were already over 18; and she could not collect a survivors' benefit from the government pension system for them. She would just get a tiny widow's pension herself when she turned 60. It would have to last her until her small national pension kicked in at 65. Hah! If she made it that far, she thought. She was 49 now. She had a few good decades ahead of her if she had a life of her own, but hers was a life of servitude, exhausting and exasperating.

When her husband died at 43, the house and farm was still in her father-in-law's name. There was nothing for her to inherit except her husband's meager personal savings and a small life insurance policy. This was just enough to bury him and help the girls go off to school in the city. It was certainly not enough for her to launch a new life of her own despite all her years of hard work. It was not enough to do much of anything.

The family had kept most of their money in their account at the agricultural cooperative, and she had no access to it. Ichiro had not been stingy. She had an ample monthly budget to run their household while he was alive. When she wanted something extra for herself or the girls, he always provided it. He just assumed—they all just assumed—that everything would proceed in an orderly way. The in-laws would die first, then he would be in charge and, as his wife, she would inherit from him.

After her husband's death, they had downsized the farm. They hired others to do the plowing for them, but it was still prosperous enough to support her in-laws very comfortably. They gave her 30,000 yen a month for herself (less than $300) and she earned a little more by selling organic vegetables from her personal garden plot at the local market. Still, it was barely enough to cover her basic minimum needs. Yet she tried to save half of it to buy presents for her grandchildren who occasionally came for the day. Her husband's family were happy to have her dependent on them and there to serve them, especially now since her father-in-law was in declining health and would likely be bedridden in a few years.

Keiko stopped her incessant analysis of her situation and went to make sure her father-in-law was all cleaned up and ready for the arrival of the visiting nurse. He was getting too feeble to travel to the main hospital 20 kilometers away, so they had signed up for the rural medical visit program. She made sure too her mother-in-law was still in the garden and had not wandered off. She wanted her to hear the nurse's explanations. She thought her mother-in-law was getting more forgetful lately. She was still her usual feisty self for now, but the thought of the years ahead made Keiko shudder again. And yet, she was lulled and cowed into moving along with this status quo game plan, controlled and regulated by the expecta-tions of others and the wider society.

Then one afternoon when her in-laws were away at-tending a local senior citizens event, everything changed. Keiko was at home watching the house and tending her garden when her cell phone rang. It was her youngest daughter Kana. Her voice sounded hoarse and cracked as she tried to speak. Keiko thought for a moment they had a bad connection. Then, she realized Kana had been crying and was making an enormous effort to stay calm on the phone.

"Can you talk now?" Kana asked.

"Yes, yes. *Oba-chan* and *oji-chan* are out for the afternoon. Now is a good time to talk. What's the matter?"

Gradually the story spilled out. It seemed Kana's husband had been having an affair with a woman from his office. She hadn't realized the affair had been going on for many months already. It had become serious. He wanted a divorce so he could marry the other woman.

Keiko was shocked. Yet she was also well aware that this was often one consequence of the Japanese corporate work culture that kept men at the office and away from home too much. In the countryside, husband and wife worked together and spent most of their time together or under the watchful eyes of the wider community. Ironically, Keiko had to credit this as one of the more positive aspects of small town life. In Tokyo, husband and wife often lived in two separate worlds and could easily drift apart or fall prey to temptations. Keiko was calm and tried to look at things logically.

"Do you want a divorce, Kana? It will be very hard for him to get one if you don't agree to it. If you want to fight it…"

"No, Mother. I don't want to keep him in my life if he no longer loves me. It would not be good for us or our daughter, and I don't trust him anymore. I despise him actually. I want him out of my life. He says I can have the condo his parents bought for us. He's going to move into her condo. I think she might be pregnant. And I can have sole custody of Kaori as long as he gets visitation rights. He says he will pay a little child support too. He can't afford much but a little."

Keiko wondered how long that would last. Men might promise child support, but there were no enforceable rules in place in Japan to penalize them if they quit paying. There were no required alimony laws in Japan either. It was all based on what conditions and what settlement the couple negotiated at the time of divorce. It was a system that often left the wife with very little.

"So we will have a place to live, but to survive I will have to go back to work. I don't mind doing that, but how am I going to raise Kaori by myself? Daycare is so expensive and so difficult to get into in Tokyo. I don't know what to do."

They talked for almost an hour. When they had finished, both women could finally see a path forward for themselves. It was suddenly clear to Keiko what had to be done. Thanks to a TV program she had come across one afternoon a year ago, she now knew just how to proceed. She reassured Kana that she would be there for her. She told her to begin exploring her job options for the autumn. It would be okay. She would move to Tokyo and take care of Kaori and the household for her. Kana would be able to take a job and be independent.

"But how are you going to do that? What about *oba-chan* and *oji-chan* and the farm?"

"Don't worry. I have a plan. I can come just after the *o-bon* holidays in August, a mere three weeks away. You just worry about having your lawyer work out that divorce agreement. Don't try to do it on your own. Make sure you have a lawyer."

And then Keiko, always one who survived by trying to look on the bright side of any adversity, commiserated with her daughter and reminded her it could be worse.

"Luckily, he was not the stalker type. What if you had wanted a divorce and he refused and tried to stalk you? You can both part cleanly and somewhat amicably now. This new woman will inherit his family and be the one who has to deal with them from now on."

Kana's husband was an only child and her in-laws had given her considerable grief since their wedding three years ago. If there was to be a divorce, this was the best possible outcome for everyone. He would be out of Kana's life completely now. Kana would be free. They would both be free.

Keiko might have thought twice about her plan had her life been different, had her in-laws been different; but it was not and they were not. Even though she had been married 25 years this past April, a date none of her in-laws even acknowledged or remembered, she really had never felt an integral part of the family unit. She was always the odd one out, the intruder, the outsider. Her own mother had warned her not to marry Ichiro because of the numerous difficulties and few rewards of marrying an eldest son in the countryside, but she had loved him. She'd been able to bear it all while he was alive and looking out for her. Now she was on her own really. She could not depend on her in-laws for much other than basic sustenance to keep her going to serve their needs. When they died, the inheritors—the sisters-in-law—would sell the land out from under her and pocket the profit. Her daughters would get her husband's share, but she would be completely on her own.

Keiko's birthday was the first week in August. Her daughters would send a card, but none of the in-laws would remember. They never did. She did all the shopping but could not treat herself to much even for her birthday. They watched the budget carefully. It was a simple, solemn life. There was only one woman in town that she could confide in and commiserate with. Akiko was an older widow. They had never talked much until they met one day at the doctor's office in a neighboring town.

Keiko hadn't seen Akiko go in ahead of her. She was busy reading a magazine, one of her rare chances to catch up on what the wider world was doing. Then she was called into the inner waiting room, a hallway outside the main examining rooms. It was designed to make those who endured long waits feel that they were getting closer and closer to their time with the doctor. The only thing was, these corridor benches were just a thin curtain away from the examining rooms. Those inside had no privacy at all and could not know who was listening in on their consultation. That day she overheard a woman who was taking care of her difficult, elderly mother-in-law confide to the doctor how exhausted she was. It was getting to be too much.

She said her own health was in decline, and she just didn't know what to do or how she could go on. Keiko could only imagine how bad the woman's situation must have been that she spoke those words to the doctor—a stranger—rather than keeping them to herself. No matter how difficult her own life could be, Keiko never mentioned the stress of her situation to anyone. Her daughters could tell, but she never made an effort to tell them. Keiko's heart ached for the poor woman, especially when she heard the doctor's response. He had just tried to console her by stating what had always been the obvious: "*Junban desu yo. Gambatte kudasai.*" *(Everyone takes their turn. Do your best.)*

He meant that life moved in cycles. It was the order of things. He was telling her that this was the way it had always been—the young took care of the elderly. Then, when they got old, their children took care of them. It was the way it was.

Keiko bristled. The elderly were now living to 98 or 100, and the young had gone off in search of their own lives. She was not sure she'd see 65 herself at this rate.

The doctor had no realization of what it was like when one's husband had been taken out of turn, when the prevailing world order had been turned upside down, and women like herself were sacrificing their last good years to care for in-laws who cared little for them. Would anyone be around to care for her? She wondered.

Keiko kept her eyes down and pretended to be nodding off when the woman came out, but she knew it was Akiko. When they met later at the cashier's counter, they nodded to each other. As they waited for their prescriptions, Keiko smiled and offered her a ride home.

"I have the car and it would be better than waiting for the bus." Akiko agreed. During that long ride home, Keiko's only really strong friendship in the town was born. Although Akiko was at least 20 years older, they spent time together now and then. They chatted when they met at some town event or activity they were required to participate in, and of which there were many. Sometimes Keiko took Akiko special dishes cooked from the vegetables in her small kitchen garden. Akiko's children had also moved away. Both women were trapped, but somehow they consoled each other and neither had totally lost hope. Keiko decided not to tell

Akiko about her plan until it had been implemented. She would write to her then.

When Keiko went to do the shopping the following week, she drove a little farther afield to the municipal office in the next town over. No one knew her there. She asked for the form she had been thinking about since that fateful afternoon a year ago when she had watched that life-altering TV program. The one-page form was very simple—name, address, the name of the town where her *koseki* family register was kept, her late husband's name and address—and that was about it. All she needed to complete the procedure was a copy of her own family register (*koseki tohon*), her driver's license for identification and her official seal. She quickly filled in the form and submitted it. The clerk said it would go into effect almost immediately. She requested a copy of the form and put it in her purse. On the way home, she stopped at a nearby convenience store and made two more copies. She suddenly felt happy and relieved. Keiko had a plan, and it was moving along on schedule. It was almost time for the final act.

Keiko spent the next two weeks silently making preparations in her mind as she tended the garden, cleaned the bath, or cooked supper for her in-laws who sat before the TV watching yet another silly comedy show. The days before the August *o-bon* visit of her sisters-in-law passed quickly, almost pleasantly. This year she actually enjoyed cleaning for them and airing their bedding and preparing a stock of food for their visit. After lunch, she went to the garden to check on the tomatoes and pluck a radish for supper. She did a quick analysis in her head of how the garden was progressing and how much she would have ready when the sisters-in-law arrived. Their husbands stayed in Tokyo to work and seldom saw their in-laws in the countryside.

The day before their arrival, she needed to get into town for a final bit of shopping. While there, she mailed two small boxes of her possessions, mostly photos and a few books, to her daughter's house. Then she finished the shopping, buying a few more pricey items to cook a really nice feast for her sisters-in-law. They arrived with plenty of souvenirs from the city as usual. Keiko actually enjoyed listening to their news and stories the first evening they were home.

Sister-in-law A's widowed mother-in-law was now in a nursing home and looked after by her eldest son. Sister-in-law B's in-laws were in wonderful health and lived with their oldest son and his wife. Both women were quite free now. Keiko was happy to hear this as it made her own decision all the more viable and much less stressful and guilt-ridden. The sisters had time for their own parents now. It was a good thing.

The spirits of the dead return home at *o-bon*. For Keiko, this year's *o-bon* was an especially poignant one, but she felt her husband was urging her on with her plan as well. The next evening, she went with the in-laws to watch the *o-bon* fireworks. For some reason, they seemed exceptionally beautiful this year, although Keiko knew they would be nothing compared to the fireworks at the farm the next day. She smiled to herself and relaxed a little. It was almost time.

Keiko was up well before dawn the next morning. Tired from the fireworks, everyone else would still be asleep for quite a while. She took the small bag she had packed—she really didn't have very much that was completely her own nor many clothes that were suitable for Tokyo—and hopped into the pickup truck at 5 a.m. Then she drove 30 minutes to the closest town with a train station.

When her guests awoke and looked for her to serve their breakfast, they found the rice ready, a pot of *miso* soup with *tofu* still warm on the stove and homemade pickled radish and eggplant from her garden neatly cut and arranged in a blue china dish. Beside it on the table was an envelope addressed to her sisters-in-law. It contained a note and a copy of an official form. The note read:

Osewa ni narimashita. Thank you for all your help over the years. Please take care of your own parents from now on. As Ichiro has been dead six years, I really need to take respon-

sibility for my own life and my children's needs now. I have left the pickup truck in the train station parking lot. The keys are under the seat. Please don't bother to search for me as you can see from this form that we are no longer connected in any legal way. Yoroshiku onegaishimasu. Keiko

The sisters gasped as they looked at the unfamiliar form and tried to absorb its meaning. Just then *oji-chan* came into the room calling out for Keiko to bring him his green tea and the morning paper. He was a little put out. Where was she anyway?

Keiko was, at that moment, happily settled in on the 5:55 a.m. local train making the hour-long trip to the main trunk line. In fact, she was just about to get off and change platforms to catch a connecting express train to Tokyo. She had written her daughter the exact date and time of her arrival. Kana would be at the station to meet her.

Meanwhile, the in-laws were still looking at the slip of paper in shock. What was this *Inzoku Kankei Shushi Todoke* anyway? One sister-in-law looked it up on her smartphone and almost fainted. "She is gone, and she is not coming back."

She read the explanation out to the others: "This is a form that the widowed can file to end all legal connections with their in-laws. It is, in a sense, a way to divorce one's in-laws, and the number of people doing so has been increasing every year."

"*Masaka* (good grief)," the other sister-in-law exclaimed. "But, but, but how could she do that? Everyone knows that a daughter-in-law takes care of her in-laws no matter what."

"Everyone thinks that, but it is not legally so. It says right here that the form goes into effect almost immediately—and this is dated two weeks ago already. It also says that her children will still have a right of inheritance as they are Ichiro's children and our blood relatives. I guess it is nice that she even told us at all. For it says some in-laws never even know the form has been filed unless they check their *koseki* family register."

"She will probably go live with one of her daughters. Maybe she will come back. Maybe we can get her to come back."

"I think it is too late. She is gone. She figured out a way to leave. Why would she come back? Besides, it says here that filing the form is a final and irreversible act. Legally speaking, you can't change your mind later. It's over."

Keiko's proud mother-in-law, if the truth be known, felt just a tad guilty. She saw the situation clearly now and had the final word: "Good riddance to her. I never really liked her much. Now I have more time for my own two daughters and can be with you more and more."

The sisters—one paler than the other—looked at each other and wondered what in the world they were going to do. Who was going to be responsible for all this now? And for the first time, they really, truly realized what the loss of their brother had meant. It had changed all their lives. They had just not realized it until now.

But, as Keiko knew, both women were clever. They began to calculate in their heads how much they could sell the farm for, how much money the elderly couple had left and where they might find a retirement home or assisted care facility in the next town that might take them. The sisters had lives to live. They could never live on a farm again. Times had changed. They had changed.

Sitting on the train to Tokyo, Keiko could merely imagine their conversations. She had been ever so slightly tempted to stay around for breakfast and present the paper herself. Once, while sitting in a doctor's waiting room, she had read a story in a women's magazine about a woman who did it that way. She got great satisfaction watching her sisters-in-law squirm, but Keiko was not that type. She was not confrontational. If she had been, she never would have lasted this long. No, she preferred the surprise approach and was happy to be far, far away when the yelling and repercussions began.

Keiko leaned back in her seat and enjoyed the warmth of the early morning sunshine on her face as she watched the scenery flash past. It was all behind her now. She felt strangely calm and relaxed. Of course, she knew she would be living her new life at the whim of her daughter who needed her help too. She would probably bear most of the burden of raising her granddaughter, but that would be joyful. It would keep her young and active. She would have a new life. And every now and then, she would take a walk in the park and breathe.

EPILOGUE

THE YEARS PASSED. Kana, who was trained as a medical secretary, found a good job with reasonable hours and working conditions. Keiko was there to take care of Kaori during the day. As she grew older, Keiko picked her up after kindergarten and made sure she got to her play groups and lessons.

Within a year of her departure, her sisters-in-law had persuaded her in-laws to sell the farm and had set them up in an assisted living facility a few towns away. Care facilities were considerably cheaper in the countryside, and the couple were in familiar surroundings. Neither of the sisters could imagine caring for them in Tokyo.

Once or twice, after she heard this, Keiko had driven quietly and unobtrusively into town to visit Ichiro's grave and leave a present for her friend Akiko, who seemed calm and serene now too. She had weathered the storm. Her mother-in-law had recently died at 101. Akiko stayed on in the house tending her garden. Her son offered to take her in, for she was 77 now, but she preferred the peace and quiet of the farm. And, as she said, she had the respect of the community now and why not stay and enjoy it a bit. During these visits, Keiko never got out to walk around or spend any time in town. It did not hold much attraction for her. Plus she knew people would talk about her, probably already did talk about her. She didn't care. She had done what was best for her own immediate family. Her daughters were all that really mattered to her now that Ichiro was gone.

When Kaori went off to school, Keiko, who knew a lot about plants, got a part-time job in a flower shop. By then, Keiko's own widowed mother had come to Tokyo to live with them. Still quite healthy, she met the school bus and helped things run smoothly while Keiko and Kana worked. Four generations of women lived together under one roof and supported each other. And sometimes on a Sunday, they all took a walk in the park together and breathed.

THE UNEXPECTED

"WELL, I'M GOING," Sarah announced as they sat in a comfortable Tokyo coffee shop for their weekly, after-work get together.

"Going? Where?"

"Home. Back to the States. It's time."

"But you have a good job, a good salary, good friends. How could you leave us?"

"You two are married. You've settled down here. I'm not interested in settling down here permanently. I want to go home and start a family. And all the unattached American guys around here are dating Japanese girls."

Jennifer had to admit most of her expat friends—male and female—were married to or dating Japanese. She knew of only one who had married a fellow expat.

Hannah agreed that Tokyo was not exactly the place to find an American guy, but she could hardly bear the thought of losing Sarah.

"You're not going too soon, are you?"

"End of the fiscal year in March."

"That soon? It's already January!"

"I gave my notice today. They were all right with it. They expect the foreign staff to come and go. They probably would have been more uncomfortable if I had wanted to stay. They said maybe they could throw some work my way after I get home. That would be nice, and it would certainly be cheaper for them if I was freelance."

The news threw a considerable damper on the party. Their Friday nights were always a special chance to relax and recharge, the salve that kept them all going for another week. Friends and acquaintances were abundant in Tokyo, but they came and went. Hannah cherished her dear old friends. They were a special treasure, and it was heartbreaking to think of losing yet another, especially Sarah. She had been there to listen to all her angst-filled doubts when she was considering whether to marry Taka. Sarah helped her plan the wedding. She, like Jennifer, was a sounding board and a valuable voice of sanity in a world that often provided incomprehensible challenges.

Jennifer, Hannah and Sarah were best friends and had been since they met as high school exchange students in Japan some ten years before. That experience had shaped their lives, and all three found it bringing them back to Japan after college. Sarah had an affinity for the language and was working as an in-house translator at a large Tokyo corporation. Jennifer, now married to Shota, a young lawyer, was a freelance proofreader/editor. Hannah followed the more traditional path and taught English.

She had started out as an AET (Assistant English Teacher) in the Tokyo suburbs. That is where she met her husband Taka.

The first time Taka took her home to meet his parents, Hannah almost reconsidered. Sarah and Jennifer had had to listen to the story of that meeting over and over:

"As soon as we sat down, Taka's father looked in the direction of his wife and declared: *oi, sake motte koi.*" If one was unaware of the meaning and intonation, it almost sounded like a poem. When she first heard her future father-in-law address his wife in this way, his voice deep and guttural and exuding not one iota of warmth, she was shocked.

"*Hey you bring me some sake.*" There was no tenderness or caring hidden beneath that command, and she wondered how her mother-in-law put up with it year in and year out. No matter how nasty his utterances, she always just smiled, assented and did what she was told. Only occasionally, she uttered a double *hai*. This 'yes, yes' response conveyed, for those who could read its meaning, a bit of impatience and irritation; but it never changed the mood in the room considerably. He was the boss and she worked her tail off for her family.

After this first meeting, Hannah had almost considered breaking up with Taka. She wondered if one day he too would end up like his father, commanding his wife with a passionless grunt. But as she got to know Taka better, she soon realized that would not be a problem. He abhorred his father's old style ways and was especially attentive to his mother's needs. He had left home at 18 to go to college on a scholarship and loans so he no longer needed to be in debt to his family. He could hardly conceal his disgust for his father, and he seemed to have only pity for his long-suffering mother.

Hannah's romance with Taka Suzuki had been intense and unexpected. Her plans were to teach in the AET program for a year or two to make some money and use her evenings to finish writing her dissertation. She had already completed the classwork for a Master's in Education at her university back home. She taught, or attempted to teach, high school classes in the daytime; but most of the teachers, lacking confidence in their own language ability, gave her little leeway in the classroom. Only with Taka was she allowed to take control of the class and actually try to teach her students something. The other teachers, wary of her and well aware of their own lack of language prowess, set up strict lesson plans. This controlled the pace and action of the class so that most of the time she was used rather like an animated tape recorder blaring out the proper English pronunciation on cue. Then she would go silent until her button was pressed again. It was very tedious and frustrating, but she tried to float above it and meditate on her dissertation during the long pauses.

Since the other teachers were all wary of her, Taka, who had studied abroad for a year, was unanimously chosen to be her immediate supervisor at the school. He had guided her through many a difficulty. By the second year, she had finished her dissertation, and they had decided to marry. So Hannah, new Master's degree in hand, found a part-time job teaching at a junior college. She was afraid that if they stayed at the same school their relationship would be found out and impact Taka's career. The truth be told, she was also very happy to leave the secondary English education system in Japan behind her.

Two years after her return to Japan, Hannah and Taka were married quietly in a small ceremony with friends. They did the paperwork necessary for recognition by both countries' legal systems at the U.S. Embassy and the local ward office during the day and had a small reception in the evening. Taka's parents did come to that dinner. Yet now, three years later, they still had not ever really accepted her as one of the family. Despite living only an hour away by train, they had only met for quick New Year visits and on a handful of other occasions since their wedding.

Taka said not to worry. When their first grandchild arrived, they would soon come around as most parents did. He said, for now, they needed to concentrate on setting up their own independent lifestyle and establish some financial stability.

Ironically, no one at the high school ever figured out their relationship. However, Taka did leave his teaching job soon after Hannah left hers but for very different reasons. It wasn't their relationship that led Taka to quit. It was the public school education system itself with its endless rules and discipline that defied a real education: Your hair is too curly, straighten it. It's not jet black, dye it. Your skirts are too long or too short. Your socks are too high or too loose. Are you wearing the proper color underwear? Take that ribbon out of your hair. And on and on it went—rules, rules, rules. And yet, there were no real, enforceable rules to deal with the *ijime* bullying, a monster more frightening and daunting than Godzilla, that had been lingering in the Japanese school system for decades and decades.

Taka had had enough after witnessing an especially egregious case of bullying. He had broken up the incident and taken the perpetrators to the principal's office and urged him to take definitive action against them, but there really was no satisfactory system in place to do so. They got off with a scolding and a reprimand and were back in school the next day. Their traumatized victim was afraid to appear for the next week, genuinely fearful they would take revenge. Eventually, Taka persuaded him to return. Then Taka found the boy's assailants—it was too sweet and naive to call them students—forcing him into a corner again. After that, the student could not be coaxed back to school, and Taka's increasingly urgent pleas to the principal went unheeded.

After all, the principal had his own standing and future promotions to consider. Who wanted to make waves? Why the media might get involved, and one of the perpetrators was the son of a well-known local business-man. Taka even went to that boy's parents but got no positive response. Instead, he was forced to face reality and realize the best way to help the victim was to get him into another school, one where student rights and dignity were more fully recognized.

Taka succeeded in finding a "free school" for the student where he could deal with the trauma, overcome his difficulties and look forward to taking the high school diploma equivalency test that would allow him to apply to colleges. These "free schools," often little more than one or two classrooms for small groups of refugees from the Japanese education system, were popping up all over Japan and were giving hope to those lucky enough to have access to them. The more open, supportive atmosphere allowed the students to learn in their own way, at their own pace and with others who were more likely to understand what they had been through. Yet Taka could not put the administrator's behavior behind him and wanted no more to do with such an education system.

Two months later, Taka Suzuki handed in his resigna-tion. The principal did not care to consider that this was his way of protesting a grossly unfair system. Rather, the principal, who had worried the independent Taka might have taken the matter to the school board, was extremely relieved and did not protest his decision to leave. Taka's secondary school teaching career was over. His protest made no waves, not even a ripple. It did not change anything. *Ijime*, the menace more frightening than Godzilla, lunged on. Yet it did change everything for Taka and Hannah. It was the beginning of a new and more satisfying phase of their teaching careers.

Taka was not about to give up. He first thought of establishing a "free school" himself, but he realized he did not yet have the resources and experience to do so. He chose instead to run a *juku,* an after-school tutoring service where he could really help students with English lessons, dispense advice and teach the academic skills they would need to get into "a suitable college." His entrance brochure specifically did not say "one of the best colleges" for he realized what was best for one was not necessarily best for another. Society, of course, did not accept that view. Several dozen universities were ranked as the best in the land and the rest as second-rate. Taka was determined to work hard to break that stereotype.

Taka ran the *juku,* managed its curriculum and advertising, and taught most of the classes. Hannah taught English there three evenings a week. She also taught part-time at a junior college three days a week and a few private English lessons. Between them, they brought in the yen equivalent of about $6,000 a month. They had bought a small condominium and were saving for a house.

They had dreams. They had hopes. They had plans for the future until the icy night of the accident when Hannah's world collapsed around her. Taka had run out to get some snacks at the local convenience store when an elderly driver, a penniless and scantily insured pensioner, confused the accelerator and the brakes and plowed into the crowd in front of the store. It was an increasingly common occurrence in Japan, but Hannah never thought that it could happen to her or impact her world. And yet, it had.

The funeral was mostly a blur. She remembered calling Sarah and Jennifer and Taka's parents. Her friends came within the hour and helped her deal with the hospital and call the undertaker the hospital suggested. Taka's parents had told her to go ahead and do that as they knew no one in the area. They arrived the next morning.

The family was not particularly religious and a secular funeral was arranged which cut the cost considerably. Had they needed to pay the costs of engaging a Buddhist priest and temple and purchasing a costly *kaimyo*, a posthumous Buddhist name, it might have more than doubled the price. As it was, the funeral would cost well over a million yen, almost $10,000.

Taka's family gave her an envelope containing just 150,000 yen and told Hannah to use this and the small envelopes of *koden* gift money, traditionally brought by those who came to pay their respects at a wake, to pay for the funeral. The accident was widely reported on TV so many students from Taka's previous high school came and all the students from the *juku* and their parents came. Taka and Hannah's many friends and colleagues came. It was a large funeral and the *koden* money did help Hannah with the costs, but it still was not nearly enough. She planned to pay the remaining 600,000 yen in fees out of her own pocket. She had no intention of asking Taka's father for anything.

Hannah really couldn't remember much of what was said or done during those three days. Then, the reality of it all came crashing down on her at the crematorium as she was told to use chopsticks to help place Taka's bones in the porcelain burial urn. The urn was sealed, placed in a wooden box and wrapped with a special white wrapping cloth so that the family could take it home with them. The whole procedure sounded macabre. In fact, while it was inescapably real and final, the Japanese custom was in a strange way also comforting. They were taking Taka home with them rather than leaving a casket to be placed in the cold ground.

Taka's father took the urn from Hannah's hands and said the family would take it home with them to place in their family altar for 49 days until it was interred in the family cemetery plot. She wanted to take Taka home with her, to their home, but she was too shocked and exhausted and overwhelmed to protest. She knew what the Japanese tradition was in this case, and she did not want to make a scene or cause an argument at Taka's funeral. So she said nothing. And then, Taka's parents and brother and sister merely bowed their farewells and walked away, leaving her standing there in shock, surrounded by her friends and the realization that life as she had known it was over.

Sarah and Jennifer found Taka's siblings rather horrid and abhorred how they somehow seemed to blame Hannah for his death. He had been hit by an elderly driver's out-of-control car, but they still seemed to blame her—if he hadn't married her, if he hadn't complicated their lives by bringing this foreign element into it.

Hannah knew that loss and grief often brought out the worst in people. Everyone dealt with shock in different ways, and she realized Taka's family too were stunned and shocked. She tried not to criticize them even when Sarah and Jennifer displayed amazement at how badly she had been treated. She didn't want to judge them on anything they said now, but it did hurt. Still, they were Taka's family, and she wanted to give them the benefit of the doubt.

Hannah realized how naive that thought had been a few weeks later when Taka's father telephoned. He said he and his wife and Taka's sister and brother would like to come to see her to talk about how Taka's inheritance would be divided. Still exhausted and in shock herself, she had not even begun to think about the paperwork and inheritance procedures. Hannah was 29. Taka just 30. They were too young to have thought of making a will. As his wife, she just assumed she would inherit the little he had. But this was not the way things worked in Japan, she soon learned.

"Divided?"

"Yes," Taka's father said rather matter-of-factly, "according to Japanese law, if a couple has no children, then the inheritance is to be divided between the spouse and the parents."

Still reeling, Hannah tried to steady her shaking voice. As calmly as possible, she said that she would be waiting for them on a Sunday afternoon two weeks hence. He suggested they could come to the condo. She gave him the address and directions as they had never visited before. Then, she rushed to call Jennifer.

"He probably just wants to see how much the condo is worth," Jennifer seethed. "We'll be over right after supper, and Shota can explain it all to you."

Shota noted that it didn't matter that Taka had not taken one yen from his father since he was 18 years old.

The Japanese inheritance system accepted his parents were entitled to one-third of his estate (or 1/6 each actually, for a total of 1/3). If they insisted on the money, Shota pointed out that there was no use fighting them. The court always ruled in this way.

Hannah was astonished. She could not believe this was how the law worked and how women could be left in such a weakened position. Shota suggested that the best she could do was to be prepared for them. She should list up all Taka's assets and propose to them how she planned to give them their share. Then, with Shota's help, they could hammer out an amicable agreement and sign off on it so that they could have all the financial matters settled well before the ten-month inheritance tax deadline arrived. The government did not give grieving survivors months and months to work through their grief. They needed to shape up and confront their new realities quickly.

Shota, Jennifer and Hannah spent the rest of the evening trying to figure out just what Taka's so-called estate would include. There was the condo. Fortunately, they had taken out one of those mortgage insurance policies that paid off the mortgage in full if the mortgage holder died. The mortgage was in Taka's name only so he was the sole owner of the condo. Shota was not sure how its value would be estimated by the tax authorities as there were various ways it could be assessed for inheritance tax purposes. They would need to talk to an accountant about that, but he figured that, at current prices, the condo's value might be about 20 million yen.

And then, there was the *juku* school itself. All the paperwork for the school was also set up in Taka's name alone. The school had around 80 enrolled students who paid about 10,000 yen a month. If a suitable buyer could be found, Shota suggested it might have a resale value of two or three million yen. Taka had a bank account with about four million yen in it. He also still had about 2.5 million yen in student loan debt. The car was in his name, and then there was the school equipment and a few other miscellaneous possessions. In total, Shota estimated that the estate was worth somewhere around 24 to 27 million yen. So if she needed to give one-third of that to his parents, she had to come up with about eight or nine million yen for them.

Hannah was flabbergasted. Where was she going to get that amount of money and still be able to start over again on her own? That was slightly more than the total of her own personal savings, and Taka had always been adamant about her keeping her own savings as a financial safety net for herself.

At least, the threshold for inheritance tax for three inheritors was 48 million yen so she was safe there. (The first 30 million yen and six million yen per inheritor were exempt from inheritance tax.) There would be no inheritance tax burden to worry about, but how was she going to come up with the eight or nine million yen settlement for his parents? Both Taka and Hannah had a small one-million yen life insurance policy (with each other as the beneficiary) as part of the private health insurance coverage they had taken out to supplement their national health insurance. She planned to use that to help pay for the rest of the funeral and hospital costs and other miscellaneous expenses. His parents had seemed all right with leaving her to pay for all that. It felt somehow like they were vultures swarming down to demand their share of the plunder. She didn't want to think that way, but it was hard not to.

Shota and Jennifer prepared to go. It was getting late and Shota had to be in court the next morning. As they left, Jennifer hugged her, pressed a copy of *The Expat's Guide to Growing Old in Japan* into her hands, and promised to be back the next evening with Sarah to help her figure things out. After all, she had only ten days to prepare for her in-laws' visit.

Hannah started reading the book as soon as they left and found so much that she hadn't known. She stayed up half the night finishing it. She realized that what her friends said was true. Without children or a will, the court would decree that his parents were entitled to one-third. Even if there had been a will, his parents could likely invoke the *iryubun* system and get at least a 1/6 share of the estate.

The *iryubun* system was a mechanism to provide for families so that they could not be completely excluded from the deceased's Will. Even if a man made a perfectly legal will leaving his estate to charity, his wife and children who, without a will, would have each received half, could protest the will via the *iryubun* system. By invoking this system, the charity would receive half, and the wife and children would each get a quarter of the estate for themselves. No wonder so many people didn't bother making wills in Japan. Where there was a Will, there was not always a way. It was all both fascinating and a little shocking.

Hannah got little sleep that night and spent the following day trying to figure things out on her calculator. She did not want to run the *juku* alone. So maybe she could sell that, but it wouldn't bring in enough money. If she sold the school and gave them the profit from that and all the cash left in Taka's bank account after the student loans were paid off, and the car, maybe they would settle for that, but she doubted it.

Of course, the easiest way to come up with the money would be to sell the condo, but then where would she live? She would have to find a place to rent, not an easy task for a lone foreigner in Japan. She also would have to ask someone to be her rental lease guarantor. She didn't want to do that either. Besides, even if she did all that, she would still have to come up with a million yen or so for the deposit and *reikin* (gift money) many landlords required renters to pay upfront. Plus the high rent in Tokyo would quickly eat into any money she got from the sale of the condo. Keeping the condo and school and giving his parents most of her own savings seemed equally untenable. The idea of being in Japan without a financial safety net was downright scary.

It was a quandary. She had no idea what to do. Then suddenly, the answer came to her. The school was Taka's dream. She was busy enough teaching at the junior college and the private lessons. The condo was only a home because Taka was there. At last she knew what to do.

By the time Sarah and Jennifer arrived that evening, Hannah had a plan. Taka's parents could have it all. It was never about money for her. It was Taka that kept her in Japan. It was Taka that made the separation from her family and friends back home bearable. The tiny condo was suffocating. The school was a responsibility she did not want or need. Had she ever been accepted as a part of his family, she might have felt responsible or inclined to stay on and help out, but she had not been and she would not be. Her period began three days after the funeral making it clear there was no chance of a pregnancy, no chance of having his child. There was nothing left to cling to in his world.

*   *   *

SARAH AND JENNIFER were shocked. "Maybe you can work out some sort of payment plan or something with them. You don't want to give them everything. That's just crazy," Jennifer warned.

"Yes, you've got to think about this, Hannah. They say one should never make big decisions right after a loss. You need time to calm down and recover from the shock," Sarah cautioned.

"I know what I'm doing," Hannah insisted. "I've gone over it again and again. I have spent all night and all day thinking about it."

"Which is just why you should wait until you are calmer. You are exhausted now and can't think straight," Jennifer urged.

"She's right, Hannah. We're your best friends. You know we want what is best for you and will back you whatever you do, but this is not in your best interests. If you give them everything, where will you live? How can you support yourself?"

"I'm going home, Sarah. Like you, I've had enough. It's time."

Now Jennifer was in tears. She didn't know if she could stand it if both her best friends left. Things were unraveling fast for everyone.

"I've decided to go home and start over. I have been able to save quite a lot these last three years. I'll manage. I'm quite lucky. Taka was so wise about our finances. He encouraged me to always keep my own earnings in my own bank account. I chipped in a bit for food and utilities now and then, but my money was basically my own. And Taka paid me for teaching at the *juku*. He wanted to keep everything business-like. I didn't invest any of my savings in the *juku* project or the condo. And I won't lose all the pension money I've been paying into the Japanese system either because there's a totalization agreement with the US that allows me to transfer my credits back into the U.S. Social Security system."

Sarah knew this was true as she had begun looking into the paperwork to move her pension credits too.

"Personally, I have not lost anything financially. I'm all right that way, but I've lost Taka, the most colossal loss of my life." And then the tears began to flow: "I don't know what I'm going to do without him, but I know it is better to put Japan behind me. I need to go home to mourn in peace."

Both friends hugged and consoled her, but neither Sarah nor Jennifer could persuade her to reconsider her options or stay on in Japan. She had decided.

Two days later, Hannah visited Shota's office and filled out all the necessary paperwork to put her plan into action including an application informing the Family Court of her intent to decline to be an inheritor, to give up all rights to the estate. This process was called *hoki suru* in Japanese, but it had to be done within three months of the death. Hannah had filed the forms in plenty of time. The *hoki suru* process was a tactic usually employed by those who wanted to avoid inheriting debt. It was an escape hatch for those who faced inheriting a relative's outstanding debts or liabilities as well as their assets. To be on the safe side, Shota also advised her to file an *Inzoku Kankei Shushi Todoke,* the simple, one-page form that would dissolve her relationship with her in-laws. They would now no longer have any legal connection.

It was very upsetting for Shota, many months later, when he realized that he might have been able to do more for Hannah. If he had had a few more years of legal experience under his belt back then, he would have known to tell her about the government's *Jidosha Songai Baisho Ho.* It was the law that provided compensation to victims of vehicular accidents caused by unknown perpetrators or the uninsured. Perhaps, it might have provided her with some money she could have used to help pay off Taka's parents. When he confessed this to Hannah a year later, she comforted him and explained she had no regrets. It had all turned out the way it was supposed to in her mind.

After all the official paperwork was organized, Hannah spent the rest of the week sorting through Taka's things and organizing his personal papers—his official seal, his pension booklet, the school accounts and student roster, his bank books, condo mortgage forms, driver's license, college loan forms and other relevant items. His whole life sat there before her neatly lined up on the kitchen table. She went through his personal items too and chose a few things that reminded her of him and happily shared memories. She packed those in a small treasure box she intended to take back to the States with her.

When the Sunday of his parents' visit arrived, she was prepared, confident and amazingly relieved. Shota and a tax accountant from his firm were there waiting with her as Taka's parents and brother and sister arrived. It was unusual they all came, and Shota wondered what would have happened if he was not there. It would have been very hard for Hannah to deal with them all on her own.

Shota smiled serenely as he pulled out his business cards and gave one to Taka's father and another to his mother. Then he formally introduced himself and took over the conversation so it all flowed smoothly in Japanese.

"Mrs. Suzuki has asked me to be here today as her lawyer to explain her wishes to you and to settle matters."

"Her lawyer?" Taka's father looked miffed and very surprised to learn she had one. "I wasn't aware that we needed to bring lawyers."

Shota continued: "Taka was the mortgage holder of this condo, and the title holder of the *juku* business, owner of the car and a bank account worth 4 million yen. He also had 2.5 million yen in student loan debt still left to be paid. Mrs. Suzuki has provided me with all this paperwork as well as his pension booklet, official seal and other papers necessary for settlement of the estate."

Taka's father seemed to relax somewhat after hearing how much Taka had accumulated. Shota continued:

"Mrs. Suzuki wishes to relinquish her right to inherit in this case and has already filed the forms to do so with the Family Court. Therefore, all of Taka's assets will go to his remaining heirs. As his parents, you will each get one half of his estate. I can carry out the paperwork for you, or perhaps you would prefer to engage a lawyer of your own choosing to settle the estate. It is entirely up to you."

Taka's father could not quite fathom what was going on, but he said he would engage his own lawyer to deal with the matter.

"Fine," Shota replied. "Mrs. Suzuki has decided to return to the United States. She has packed up her things and will be moving out of the condo today by 5 p.m. We will leave the keys with you then. This will be her last formal meeting with you as she has also filed an *Inzoku Kankei Shushi Todoke* and thus is no longer related to you in any way. If there are any further matters to be discussed, they can be discussed via my office. You have my card."

Taka's parents and siblings were all quite aghast. They had expected to have to fight this outsider for their share, and now they were getting it all. Their satisfaction was overwhelmed by the shock of Hannah giving it all up. It was incomprehensible to them, and, in a way, so noble of her. Yet, they were not inclined to give her any praise. So it was awkward for them, financially satisfying but still a bit awkward.

Her father-in-law offered a gruff *wakarimashita* (I understand). Her mother-in-law turned to Hannah with a look of pity on her face and consoling eyes. Mr. Suzuki picked up the papers, bankbooks and seal and put them in his briefcase. As he prepared to leave, he said they would go out to eat and return at 5 p.m. Obviously, they needed some time alone to process this surprising set of circumstances. Taka's father put on his shoes, bowed his head ever so slightly and was gone. His wife, trailing behind him, turned and bowed more deeply but said nothing. Taka's sister and brother followed them out the door. As they left, his sister turned to Hannah: "I think you are doing the right thing to leave Japan. After all, you are American."

At exactly 5 p.m., they returned. Hannah was ready with her bags near the door. Sarah and Jennifer and Shota were there too to help her move them to Sarah's apartment where she would stay until her college classes finished up. Hannah thanked Taka's family for having let her share their wonderful son. And with great dignity, she walked out the door, leaving them all standing there dumbfounded in the condo living room.

Hannah would always be the outsider. She accepted it, surrendered to it and walked away feeling like a huge burden had been lifted from her shoulders. She was now free to mourn in peace, free to treasure her memories without tarnishing them with the nastiness of her father-in-law's greed for his son's self-made wealth. She wondered if they might feel a little guilty, but she doubted it. They were not likely to feel anything towards her. They got what they were entitled to and more, and she was gone from their lives.

Hannah was not completely noble. She did feel she had gotten a bit of revenge. Beside the justification of having given them more than even they wanted, they would have to pay off the student loan, deal with the condo and probably sell it. They would have to manage the school. They were not at all capable of doing so. If they were lucky, they might quickly find a buyer willing to take over the *juku*. If not, they would probably have to scrap it and settle accounts with the students. There was a lot of paperwork ahead of them.

Hannah had handed in her resignation at the junior college effective as of the end of March. Just 10 weeks after the accident, she was on the plane with Sarah heading home. She thought back to that day in January when Sarah announced she was leaving. Never in her wildest dreams had Hannah imagined that she might be going with her.

As the plane rolled onto the tarmac at Dulles, Sarah turned to Hannah and smiled: "We're back. Welcome home."

Hannah didn't feel at home. Even though she had been away just five years, everything seemed strange and different. She realized she didn't know the expected code words that kept society moving smoothly. She didn't know what to say to waiters...er servers...nor how much to tip anymore. She didn't know what were comfortable levels of politeness. She tended to nod and bow slightly and garner strange looks. She still carried cash in her wallet and didn't know how to call an Uber. And she had no recent credit rating and no insurance yet. Thank goodness, she had her family for support and Sarah. She was going through the same things. They could commiserate and help each other readjust.

As time passed, Hannah relearned how to live in her world. She was still young and tough and smart. She found a teaching job. Over the course of the year, she gradually felt at home again and free from so many of the restrictions that constrained her life in Japan. She had started over again somehow. She had made the right decision. As the first anniversary of Taka's death passed, she wondered how his family had marked the occasion.

A few weeks later, she heard from Jennifer that Taka's mother had saved Shota's business card and consulted his office on several occasions. She had also asked Shota and Jennifer to translate a letter to Hannah for her. It read:

Dear Hannah, How are you? I hope you are well and re-starting your life in your own country. I'm sure you miss Taka terribly, as I do, but we must go on. The cherry blossoms are blooming, and the days are growing warmer. It is a good time to start a new life.

I wanted to write and thank you for your generous and selfless decision to refuse Taka's inheritance although you certainly had a right to most of it. My husband was going to bank it all, but I remembered what your lawyer said about half of it now being mine. I contacted him, and he offered to represent me in the estate settlement.

Taka's father was, of course, very shocked by my decision to want to manage my own money and clueless about my feelings. Now that the children were all raised, I wanted to spend my last years in peace. This inheritance was the way I could do so.

After the settlement, I divorced my husband and have resettled in a small apartment of my own now. Taka's father has to serve himself his own sake and take care of himself now. Otherwise, he doesn't seem to miss me much. And I

am, for the first time in many years, almost happy; although
I will never be completely happy without my Taka.

I just wanted to write and thank you and let you know
my new address should you ever need to contact me. Again,
thank you for your kindness. It has given me back my life.
Please take care of yourself.

Yoshiko Suzuki

Hannah had tears in her eyes as she read the letter. Then she smiled thinking how happy Taka would have been with the decision she made. She had made the right choice, and it was a positive, life-changing decision for her mother-in-law too. She had done the right thing and enabled her to have the life that Taka had so wanted to give her himself one day.

The following Sunday would mark their fifth wedding anniversary. They were making plans for a fourth anniversary trip the day he died. This year, she planned to make a banana cake—Taka loved her banana cake—and spend the day hiking in the forest with Sarah. Hannah needed some quiet time to contemplate her past and the unknown future. She would walk in the forest and celebrate her memories of their life together. Then, she would move forward and maybe even think of dating again. Taka would want her to get on with her life.

The spring air was fresh and crisp and the first crocuses were pushing through the forest floor. A new season, a season of rebirth, was dawning. It would mark a new beginning for both Hannah and her mother-in-law, and maybe Taka too would be reborn somewhere and have another chance at life himself. She wasn't sure she really believed in reincarnation, but who knows? It was a pleasant thought anyway, and she held on to it for the rest of the afternoon.

THE HONDA BROTHERS

HIRO HONDA WAS the kind of fellow you just couldn't forget. This was partly because of his name and partly because of his style. He had a happy-go-lucky way about him that was both endearing and annoying. It made one envious of how he could sail through life without worrying or stressing out. It made him very likeable to his friends and a bit of a concern to his brother Ichiro.

Being the eldest, Ichiro had taken over the family business and diligently carried out his responsibilities for the family graves and the genealogical records that allowed them to trace their family tree back ten generations.

Both men were rather tall and thin. Physically, the family resemblance was strong. Personality-wise, the brothers were about as different as two people could be. Ichiro was ten years older. Born in 1947, during the great postwar baby boom, he still had vague memories of what Japan looked and felt like in the early 1950s. He had watched as his parents struggled to survive. Under his grandmother's care and influence, he was taught respect for the old ways and the responsibilities of an eldest son.

Ichiro grew up knowing he had a role to carry out for the family.

Hiro was born ten years later in 1957 when Japan had begun regaining its strength and vitality. Hiro's first memories were of the excitement of the Tokyo Olympics of 1964, which marked Japan's real return to the international stage. Hiro was rather like the Olympics—a bit splashy, flashy, full of pride and hope for a new era. He was ready for the good times, and Hiro did enjoy his good times.

While Ichiro took over the family coffee shop in Tokyo, Hiro went to college and became a *salaryman.* For a while, Hiro tried to do all the right things too. He found a wife at the company and worked long hours for the security of a salary, pension plan and twice yearly bonuses. Yet, he wasn't happy. Hiro had an artistic side and dreamed of becoming a freelance photographer. He wanted to travel the world, take pictures and sell them to the highest bidder in Japan's bustling mass media world of the 1980s.

When Hiro began threatening to leave his job, his wife decided to leave him. With no children to worry about, they divorced amicably. Within a year, Hiro did leave his job and lived on his severance pay for a few months. Then their father died. Under the Japanese inheritance system, the spouse and children were to share the inheritance fifty-fifty. However, Hiro signed an agreement declining his share of the building and business and taking a cash settlement instead.

Hiro used his inheritance to travel the world and take photos. He even made a bit of a name for himself in the freelance photography field. For over a decade, he sold enough to keep himself eating and socializing with the editors who occasionally threw more work his way. For a few years, he was even quite in demand. But as he aged, he found it harder to maintain the pace and a sharp eye for the kind of photos the market demanded.

After the turn-of-the-century, Hiro gradually came to realize he really didn't like the photography of the new digital age all that much. He found he was having a harder time keeping up with technical trends in the industry, and many of the contacts who had given him assignments were retiring.

When their mother died, the Honda brothers had to divide the estate. As the eldest son, Ichiro's half of the inheritance included the coffee shop and the suburban Tokyo land it was built on, while Hiro got quite a hefty amount of cash. Used carefully and supplemented by an occasional loan from his brother, it was enough to keep Hiro going for a few more years.

Gradually, Hiro was overwhelmed by the ever-changing computer technology and expensive gadgets and lost interest in his art completely. He was not the hardy professional with advanced computer skills that the field now demanded. By 2019, when he was sixty-two, Hiro considered himself retired and took his little government pension. It barely paid for food, and he certainly had never saved much. He found he now had to borrow money from Ichiro more often than before.

Meanwhile, Ichiro had adapted the coffee shop to the new ways of the world. He experimented with all sorts of apps and services, set up free Wi-Fi, work space corners and booths that kept the place full all day long.

Hiro was not the worrying type, in part, because he felt he could always count on his brother. He thought of Ichiro as his insurance policy, especially after Ichiro was diagnosed with Stage IV cancer.

Although the inheritance law was full of bureaucratic rules and legalese, Hiro had whittled it down to simpler, more understandable terms. He called it the one-half, one-third, one-quarter rule. Generally speaking, this meant when a person dies in Japan without a Will, his spouse and children share the estate fifty-fifty. If there are no children, the spouse gets two-thirds and the deceased's parents are entitled to one-third. If no children or parents exist, the spouse gets three-fourths and the deceased's siblings share one-fourth.

Hiro believed this rule of thumb was based on the concept that no one amasses a fortune alone without the support of others and generations of family struggle and toil. So it seemed natural to Hiro that all the family should share in the inheritance too. And since he would be the only survivor of his family, he felt he was certainly entitled to it all. Hiro had not spent any time contemplating what would happen if Ichiro had made a Will. The lackadaisical Hiro hadn't quite done all his homework.

Since Ichiro had never married, he was pretty much on his own in his final years. Hiro checked in on him occasionally, but he did not move back into the family home above the coffee shop even after his brother took ill. When Ichiro's condition began to deteriorate, the coffee shop was temporarily closed, and he was hospitalized. Hiro occasionally visited him. He felt bad for his brother, but he realized he was of limited physical or moral support. Hiro was not a bad sort. In his own way, he loved and appreciated his brother, but none of those feelings rose above his great preoccupation with himself.

As Ichiro's condition worsened, he realized he was gazing at the golden leaves of the gingko trees in the nearby park for the last time. He told Hiro where the family history records were located. He gave him the name of the lawyer to contact after his death and the number of the funeral director. Ichiro had paid in advance for a simple *kazoku so*. Such small family funerals were becoming quite common nowadays.

A few weeks after the funeral and cremation, Hiro made an appointment with the lawyer and calmly appeared at his office at the appointed time. He was ready to claim his inheritance and already calculating the value of the land. He thought it could be quite substantial. The inheritance tax probably would be sizeable too. Yet he figured he'd still have a tidy sum left.

Hiro arrived at the office in quite a good humor, but he adopted the appropriately subdued and solemn demeanor of the recently bereaved as he entered the lawyer's office. The accountant was there too, but neither of the men were particularly friendly or deferential. The accountant had been doing Ichiro's books for decades, and both men were quite well aware of the long list of personal loans to Hiro that had not been repaid over the years.

Ichiro's lawyer had in his possession Ichiro's Last Will and Testament which specified that Hiro should take charge of the family history documents and graves. For this, he would receive a small yearly stipend to cover the costs of cemetery maintenance. The Tokyo coffee shop and the land it sat on was left to Mrs. Kawasaki, the kind lady who ran the homemade *wagashi* (Japanese sweets) shop next door.

The shop featured all sorts of bean jam-paste and rice-flour creations. Some were artistically done, but most were just very tasty, down-to-earth, home-cooked fare like *ohagi* (bean jam-covered rice balls), *kashiwa mochi* (chewy rice cakes wrapped in oak leaves) and various *dango* (rice dumplings on a stick). Mrs. Kawasaki charged reasonable prices and had a lot of customers. She was always offering extra "service" too, so her profits were not great although the rent was high.

The Will stated that she was a kind and caring neighbor who was just a good friend, a rarity in these lonely days.

"What? Mrs. Kawasaki is just a neighbor." Hiro couldn't believe Ichiro would leave everything to her.

The lawyer also read a personal letter from Ichiro to Hiro that warned him not to cause a fuss or start any rumors among the neighbors. It read:

"I made sure everyone in the neighborhood knew we were just platonic friends and that Mrs. Kawasaki was someone who made me a dish of food or bean-paste sweets now and then. She was just someone who cared that I was alive—no more than that. Everyone in the neighborhood can vouch for her kindness. They know she was just as good and reliable a friend to them as she was to me, and I would like to reward that selfless spirit of friendship. Despite her own difficulties, she has had the generosity of spirit to worry about me and think of all her neighbors despite her own problems. I really do want to reward her goodness."

The lawyers confirmed the land was valuable. As the only heir, she would have to sell it quickly to pay the inheritance tax within the ten-month limit. After taxes and legal fees, Ichiro had hoped she would receive the yen equivalent of about $300,000.

Hiro's shock was overwhelming. Why was he being shunned for a mere neighbor now? He just couldn't understand it. He hardly knew how to reply. Yet he still had his wits about him enough to ask: "But what about my *iryubun* share?"

He was referring to the Japanese system of allowing relatives to inherit a part of an estate even if there was a will that disinherited them and left everything to a charity or someone else. The inability to completely write off one's blood relatives was probably one of the reasons many Japanese didn't bother to write a will at all.

But the lawyer shook his head and explained. "It is true if there was no will, you would inherit everything as there are no other relatives. Even with a Will, the *iryubun* system would apply if you were the child, or spouse, or even the parent of the deceased. However, you are a brother, and the simple fact is that when there is a valid will, the *iryubun* system does not apply to you. Siblings are the only first-degree blood relatives one can successfully write out of one's will in Japan. You have no right to anything."

And a wise law it is, the lawyer thought to himself as Hiro Honda grabbed the corner of the table for balance and slouched into his chair in complete shock and disbelief. His old age insurance policy had just evaporated in front of his eyes.

"What am I going to do now?" he muttered.

"Well, I suppose you could get a job or a Loto 6 lottery ticket," the lawyer replied without an iota of sympathy.

Instead, Hiro bought himself a large two-liter bottle of cheap *shochu* liquor and drank for three days. He felt his sorry fate was certainly justification for doing so. He was just awakening from a blurry weekend of trying to forget what he could never forget when the phone rang.

He had in no way begun to deal with the shock of his new reality. Yet the astonishing news he was about to receive was a shock so huge, he could barely fathom it. The lawyer too found it profoundly upsetting and unbelievable. He had never handled such a baffling case before. Still, it was his duty to inform Hiro of his fate.

The disgusted lawyer sighed, bit his lip, and clenched his phone as he made the distressing call. The attorney had thought that Hiro Honda got just what he deserved when his brother wrote him out of his Will. He thought Hiro was at last paying the price for his free and gallivanting lifestyle. The hardworking lawyer found that a very satisfying thought. Yet now, it was his job to phone Hiro and tell him he was to have his cake and eat it too, so to speak. It was all dessert for Hiro from here on out, and it was galling that it was his job to convey the good news.

The hungover Hiro immediately sobered up when he heard the neighbor who had inherited Ichiro's estate didn't want it. The estate would go to Hiro after all.

Mrs. Kawasaki planned to file the papers to relinquish any right to the estate, a process called *hoki suru* in Japanese. This had to be done within three months of a death. It was an option usually reserved for people trying to free themselves from inheriting the deceased's debts. For Japan was one of those countries where an individual could inherit debt. It was always essential to know the financial situation of the deceased before accepting any Japanese inheritance.

To the lawyer, it all seemed a cruel irony. Despite all the serious people plodding on like industrious ants in this world, why should Hiro, a languishing grasshopper, be so blessed? Yet it was true.

Mrs. Kawasaki was a widow who had raised her only son on her own. He now had a very lucrative job with a high-tech company that had relocated to a distant suburban location where land prices were cheaper. He had built himself a house and found another small house nearby for his mother. In a few more years, she would be a useful babysitter. Mrs. Kawasaki was thrilled about the move and told the lawyer she was closing up the shop and leaving Tokyo the following month.

The attorney did not understand why she didn't want to move on with her newfound wealth in tow, but she did not. She didn't want the bother. She was happy the way she was and wise enough to realize good health, family, friends and a modestly comfortable home were life's true treasures.

The lawyer tried to explain the estate was unencumbered. Ichiro owed no money to anyone. He had not served as guarantor for anyone either, a dangerous move that often left one with a mountain of another person's debts. The estate was clear, and it would all go to her. She reiterated she did not want it and had no intention of accepting it. She said she had no use for it. She felt it should go to Mr. Honda's brother who seemed to need it.

Mrs. Kawasaki did make one small request for *katami*. This was the Japanese custom of giving friends and relatives some small item that had belonged to the deceased person, a keepsake to remember them by. In this case, she requested a picture of Mr. Honda and a set of five, delicately crafted, porcelain tea cups that he kept in the coffee shop for his favorite guests. He had often served her a cup of Earl Grey tea in one of those cups when she dropped in, and he made a lovely cup of tea. It had cheered her many times.

Mrs. Kawasaki also confessed that there had been several times when Ichiro, out of the goodness of his heart, had kindly helped her son with his college education. They had never requested aid, but her son had worked in the coffee shop part-time during school vacations. Every winter, Ichiro gave him a yearend present. One year when the economy was bad and she wondered how she would pay her son's college tuition, Ichiro's yearend present to her son was a box of warm socks—with half-a-million yen nestled inside. Ichiro was a real Santa Claus that year. It had been enough to take care of most of the next term's tuition.

Mrs. Kawasaki had been very grateful for his kindness. Yet he would never accept repayment, saying it was a yearend gift he wanted to give. Besides, he had no real family of his own to spend his money on—except Hiro, of course.

Hiro was quite touched by these—to him—alien concepts of generosity and gratitude. For a moment, he thought that, perhaps, he should run the coffee shop for a while too and help all of those his brother had. However, the inheritance tax was looming, and that was not really an option. He would have to sell the land—a fate that hit many family-run businesses in the capital.

For now though, Hiro had moved into the building and was slowly cleaning it out. He also was realizing what a good person his brother had been and what his brother saw in Mrs. Kawasaki. She was a kind, generous, compassionate and completely selfless woman, not at all greedy.

Hiro prepared a framed photo of Ichiro and the box of tea cups. He carefully placed them in a dark purple *furoshiki* wrapping cloth and presented them to Mrs.

Kawasaki as they said their goodbyes on the day she left the neighborhood. He wished her well, and they bowed formally. She took a few steps and turned to nod her head to him one last time. Then she walked away from a handsome fortune that could have been hers.

Hiro stood, still bowing ever so slightly, and watched as she made her way down the shopping street and gradually blended into the crowd. He felt he owed her a proper farewell. Hiro had never met a person who was so selfless and generous of spirit before. He wondered if he would ever meet one again. He doubted it.

Hiro was not the only one watching Mrs. Kawasaki leave. Ichiro, recently reborn as a Japanese bobtail cat with one brown ear and one black ear, plopped down near the coffee shop so he could see what would happen as Mrs. Kawasaki claimed her fortune. Although he always knew she was kind and generous, he was completely thrown off by her refusal to become rich.

He had no interest in what Hiro would do with the estate, but he couldn't quite part with Mrs. Kawasaki. If the truth be told, he had been in love with her for a very long time, but he was too shy to tell her. And he feared if he did tell her, he might lose her friendship.

As she departed, he trailed her at a safe distance and watched her board the train to the town where he knew her son lived. Then he made his way there himself, being careful to avoid animal control crews or any kind old ladies who might want to capture and adopt him. It took him several weeks to complete the journey. By that time, Mrs. Kawasaki was settled in her little house.

Ichiro hung around the back door until Mrs. Kawasaki took pity on him, which he knew she would. Eventually, she adopted and registered him, got him his shots and a nice collar. She named him Bunta after a handsome Japanese actor of her youth who specialized in tough guy roles. And thus, Bunta/Ichiro took up residence with Mrs. Kawasaki. His dream had come true.

THE PET STORE

MRS. KAWASAKI, WHO was always kind and generous, settled easily into her new suburban surroundings. She was soon hosting the neighborhood ladies for afternoon teas featuring her famed *wagashi* sweets.

One afternoon in April, her guests were sitting around Mrs. Kawasaki's dining room table drinking delicate cherry blossom tea and eating delicious *sakura-mochi*. These were soft, pink, bean jam-filled rice cakes that were wrapped in fragrant, salted cherry tree leaves. Mrs. Kawasaki made them herself and the ladies just raved about them.

Her guests included Mrs. Nishi and Mrs. Higashi, who lived across the street on opposite ends of the block, Mrs. Tanaka, who lived next door, and Jennifer, who lived two houses down.

When the ladies realized an American who spoke fluent Japanese had moved into the neighborhood, it was big news. So naturally, Mrs. Kawasaki invited Jennifer over for a cup of tea to meet some of the other local ladies. They chatted amicably about the neighborhood garbage collection rules, the best grocery stores and life experiences—mostly Jennifer's.

They learned her husband, Shota, was a bilingual attorney who had set up a small law practice nearby. Jennifer explained that after her two best friends suddenly returned to the United States, she had lost interest in big city life and had been happy to move to the suburbs. Shota's clientele were largely Japanese or foreign residents who needed a bilingual lawyer who could understand their problems. He dealt mainly with wills, divorces, deeds and various types of immigration forms and entanglements.

The ladies discovered Jennifer was an editor who worked from home, and they had no children nor any plans for them until Shota's law practice was stable. And let's see what else—Jennifer's parents lived in Ohio, and she had been in Japan off and on since she came as a high school exchange student well over a decade ago. And, oh yes, she had parakeets named Lemon and Lime.

The neighborhood ladies learned quite a lot about Jennifer that afternoon although they were not nearly as forthcoming with their own background stories. They knew the perils of revealing too much and becoming the topic of the neighborhood gossip mill, but foreign residents were not allowed such privacy. Sooner or later, everyone would know just about everything they did in public. Sometimes, the neighbors might know more than the expats themselves remembered. Neighbors could often recall just when and where they had last seen them and what they were buying in the supermarket or doing at the post office at that time. So savvy, long-time expats like Jennifer gradually figured out just how much information they had to reveal while still trying to maintain a tiny bit of privacy.

At an appropriate pause in the conversation, Mrs. Tanaka wondered if Jennifer-san might consider teaching the little group English conversation.

Jennifer was a very cool, calm and clever sort. She had obviously come prepared for just this moment. After a bit of tactful hemming and hawing, she made a suggestion.

She explained that actually she was not an English teacher and had no degree or experience in the field. What she didn't say was that she was also wary of dealing with any activity involving the exchange of money for services rendered among such near neighbors. How would she ever stop teaching if she wanted to quit? She couldn't feign illness when the students lived right next door. She wanted no hard feelings or further indebtedness if things didn't go well.

Evidently, Jennifer had also lived in Japan long enough to know how things could escalate both in terms of human relations, misunderstandings and gift exchanges. In fact, she had lived in Tokyo long enough to sense what was coming long before she was invited over. So she came

prepared not to fall into any well-intentioned but potentially stressful entanglements.

Jennifer suggested that instead of a stiff and formal
class, maybe they could all just meet for chats and call it
an informal neighborhood circle. It could be a once-a-
month get together, and one could speak in English or
Japanese—no restrictions. The others could help explain
if someone got confused. This way, if someone—like
her—couldn't come sometime, it would not be a big deal.
The group could continue on its own. It was a very clever
and wise solution, and the monthly afternoon teas became
an event they all looked forward to—even Bunta, who
refused to be petted and sat glued to his spot at Mrs.
Kawasaki's feet at all times. Everyone always remarked
how loyal and devoted he was. And on the days when
Mrs. Kawasaki cheerfully served the ladies Earl Grey tea
in her special porcelain tea cups, he purred with content-
ment.

At the group's next get-together in May, Mrs Kawasaki
served delicate *wagashi* designed to look just like hydrangea
flowers. Everyone complimented her on how beautiful
and delicious they were and wanted to know how she
made them.

She explained how she prepared *kanten* (agar agar)
gelatin and tinted it with red and blue food coloring.
Then, she carefully mixed the *kanten* colors to create
shades of pink and purple too. Once solidified, the gelatin

was cut into tiny squares and carefully shaped and sculpted around small balls of sweet, white bean paste. In the hands of an artisan like Mrs. Kawasaki, they looked amazingly like miniature hydrangea. Beautiful and tasty, they were a refreshing summer delicacy.

As they nibbled the artistic creations, the talk turned to their pets. Mrs. Nishi had a miniature schnauzer called Elvis. Mrs. Higashi lived with her beagle Vick and Mrs. Tanaka had a cat named Yuki-chan. Jennifer mentioned that she was worried about Lemon and Lime. She wondered if they would ever produce any babies. They seemed not in the least enamored of each other.

Mrs. Higashi asked where she had purchased the birds and Jennifer explained they had bought them at Mr. Ando's pet store on the shopping street, a ten-minute walk from their homes.

"That's where I buy all of Vick's collars, you know," Mrs. Higashi noted. Vick was a very personable beagle. His only fault was that he chewed through all his collars. So Mrs. Higashi was a frequent customer at the pet store.

"I am in there quite often. In fact, the last time I was there, I heard Mr. Ando and his wife talking over by the parakeet cages. They were discussing how to match the birds up for sale since parakeets really don't like to be alone if they can help it. The couple were mixing and matching the new arrivals into colorful pairs that they thought would entice buyers. The day I was there, they had a lovely blue parakeet and a yellow one paired up."

This struck a chord with Jennifer since Lemon and Lime were naturally lovely shades of yellow and green. Yet she had always thought they did tests to make sure they were selling a male and female together. They had asked for a pair that could mate.

"Oh no," Mrs. Higashi, now suddenly quite an expert on parakeets, continued: "From what they were saying, unless you go to all the bother of doing bird DNA, it is hard to identify their sex until they are about one year old. Well, at least that's what I heard them saying."

Evidently, Mr. Ando, not schooled in veterinary medicine or ornithology and not much interested in paperwork, had just been color coordinating them. He couldn't tell a male parakeet from a female.

"Are your birds very talkative?" Mrs. Nishi asked. "I've heard male parakeets talk much more than females."

"Oh yes, they are both very, very talkative. Do you think they could both be males?"

That evening when Shota heard the story, he got suspicious, and they took the birds to the vet to find out."

And sure enough, Lemon and Lime were both males, and Jennifer despaired of ever finding mates for them at Mr. Ando's store. Instead she ordered new mates from a reputable online dealer who did DNA testing first.

Shota became leery of the Ando pet shop after that and noticed Mr. Ando had a large shed out back of the property. In late May, Shoto and Jennifer had walked past and noticed an unusual smell coming from the shed. He suspected there was something strange going on there.

Jennifer agreed. "The scent almost reminded me of the time I ran into a snake down by the river in my childhood."

"Reptiles?" Shota's interest was piqued. He was well aware of the cases of escaped reptiles that had been frightening and entertaining the country for the last few years Who would ever suspect that there were so many pythons and lizards and giant salamanders holed up, or held captive, in little walk-up apartments all over the country.

The Kanto region especially had been plagued with lost lizards, iguanas and several pythons. It was no cliche to say that many people had no idea who their neighbors were.

Shota wondered what secrets were hidden inside that shed, but he had no way to find out. Even if there were illegally imported reptiles inside, there was really not much he could do. He was well aware that it was important to cut off the illegal trade in endangered species at the port of entry since Japan had no proper penalties in place to deal with the situation otherwise.

After the animals had taken up residence in Japan, it was almost impossible to prove whether they had been smuggled in or bred here. And if they were born in Japan, they could be bought and sold without much difficulty. There were many ways to skirt the law, and the smugglers knew them all.

It would be months before the neighborhood learned that smugglers had been shipping endangered species to Mr. Ando, sometimes via package delivery service, for a very long time. Mr. Ando kept them and fed and cared for them in his back shed until a buyer for the creature was found. Then the customer picked up their purchase discreetly at Mr. Ando's store. It was a relatively smooth operation. The smugglers did not have to bother with the storage and day-to-day care of the creatures, which lessened their chances of getting caught, and Mr. Ando made a nice little side income that he did not report to the tax authorities.

Mr. Ando was such a jovial, happy-go-lucky fellow no one ever suspected he had a more nefarious side to him.

Then one day at the end of May, Mr. Ando clutched his chest, toppled over and was rushed to the hospital where he was pronounced dead of a massive heart attack. The neighborhood ladies could talk of nothing else at their June meeting, and they all assumed Mrs. Ando would continue to run the store.

At their late July meeting, the ladies enjoyed delicate chilled desserts that featured tiny bits of fruit covered in clear *kanten* gelatin and Mrs. Kawasaki's famed watermelon-flavored gelatin served in freshly carved watermelon rinds. This dessert even included tiny black beans masquerading as watermelon seeds to give the treats an impressive authenticity. The artistic delicacies were designed to cool the palate in the horrendous 90 degree heat and matching 90 per cent humidity.

Despite their luscious appearance, the soothing sweets alone were not quite enough to cool the ladies down. It was only when they learned the latest chilling news from the Ando pet shop that they forgot about the heat.

Mrs. Tanaka asked if everyone had heard that Mrs. Ando had died the previous week. They all agreed it was quite amazing the couple had died within two months of each other.

"What happened to her?" Mrs. Nishi wondered.

Mrs. Tanaka said she had heard it was a stroke, probably brought on by all the stress of the funeral, sending return presents to those who had sent their condolences, and trying to run the shop on her own.

Mrs. Tanaka had stopped by the store to pick up some supplies and found a notice on the door that said it would reopen August 10. She hoped so as she wondered where she would buy her pet supplies if it did not.

For their September meeting, Mrs. Kawasaki prepared some lovely *tsukimi dango* dumplings, a traditional autumn moon-viewing treat. Again, the main topic of discussion was the Ando pet store. The ladies were speculating as to why Mrs. Ando's younger daughter, Yumi, had taken over the store rather than her older brother Hiroshi.

"He is a *salaryman* somewhere in Tokyo, and he probably doesn't want to quit his job," Mrs. Higashi guessed.

"Or maybe the store is not profitable enough for him," Mrs. Nishi assumed.

Jennifer sat quietly and listened to the women presume and suppose. She knew what the real answer was, but she always tried to respect Shota's clients and their confidences. So she just sat back and sipped her Earl Grey tea and admired the lovely porcelain cup.

*   *   *

IT WAS LATE September before all the ladies discovered the rest of the story, the real truth that Jennifer hadn't shared that day. Mr. Ando's son, Hiroshi, had been disinherited.

While Mr. Ando was a very jolly and helpful fellow to his customers, he did have a tendency to be evasive at times. He also had a very lackadaisical attitude toward paperwork. He just hated it and never paid much attention to it if he could help it. Thus, he had certainly never bothered to make a will or anything like that.

However, he had paid for the college education of both his children. At that time, he had made them promise not to take their one-quarter shares of his estate when he died. They were legally entitled to the money, but he insisted they promise that everything was to be left to his wife, who was ten years younger than Mr. Ando. She would need the whole estate to be financially secure and able to continue running the store. The children had agreed to this plan.

After their father died, they were quite eager to put their mother at ease by quickly signing the *isan bunkatsu kyogisho* forms to settle his estate. They did this in early July.

Hiroshi was happy to do this quickly. He had a two-month, overseas business trip coming up in the autumn, and he wanted to clear away his share of the paperwork before he left. But then, just two weeks later, Mrs. Ando died.

Two deaths in such a short span of time meant the children would be re-inheriting what Mrs. Ando had just inherited. There were rules that usually helped lessen the tax burden in such cases. Still. everything would have to be settled and all the taxes due paid within ten months of Mrs. Ando's death. Otherwise, penalties would start accumulating.

As his business trip was quickly approaching, Hiroshi decided he better see a lawyer about getting the paperwork started so things could be moving along while he was gone. He didn't want to leave Yumi to deal with it all on her own. She agreed this was a good idea, and that is how Hiroshi found himself in Shota's office one morning in mid-August.

Hiroshi presented Shota with copies of the death certificates, their family register and a few other items. He asked that Shota get the process started as he would have to be away for the months of September and October.

Shota, as he told Jennifer later, looked at the papers, sighed deeply and announced: "But you are not an inheritor. You are no relation to the deceased at all."

It was then that Hiroshi made a life-shattering discovery. He was not legally entitled to any of the inheritance. Hiroshi's real mother had died when he was a baby and Mr. Ando, in need of someone to take care of him, had entered into an arranged marriage soon thereafter. The couple's marriage had been a happy one, and his sister Yumi had been born two years later.

As was often the case in Japan in those days, Mr. Ando had not told his son about this, and Hiroshi had grown up happily thinking the kind Mrs. Ando was his real mother. She was a lovely, caring lady, and he had never guessed they were not related. Then, when he was ready to go off to college, his father finally explained the situation.

However, Mr. Ando, being so averse to paperwork, had never bothered to have the second Mrs. Ando adopt

Hiroshi. (This was called *yoshien gumi* in Japanese.) So
when she died, Hiroshi discovered that legally she was no
relation to him at all, and he had no right to inherit any of
her estate.

It didn't matter that it was actually his father's estate.
Legally speaking, it was now hers, and he was not a blood
relative. And if you are not a spouse or blood relative in
Japan, your chances of inheriting anything are close to nil.
Legally, the estate would all go to Yumi. Hiroshi was
completely disinherited.

"I really don't know why," Shota lamented, "people
don't learn the basics of the inheritance law. They should
teach it in high school. It would save all future heirs and
the legal profession a lot of stress and trouble."

Hiroshi, who was not yet married, had a good job and
a modest but sufficient income. He was not really interested in the pet store. It certainly was not a big
moneymaker. Losing the store was not a huge financial
blow to him. Plus he would not have wanted to sell the
building that housed the shop and the living quarters
above. It was where they had grown up and his sister still
lived. He had just imagined that one day in the distant
future the property would be sold, and his half would
have come in handy for the education of his future
children.

Hiroshi was not a greedy person. In fact, his name
meant generous and tolerant in Japanese. So he accepted

that his own ignorance, fate and his father's carelessness were responsible for the situation.

He did think his sister should have offered him something of the estate since he had acted as the eldest son all these years, but she did not seem at all inclined to do that. Having not much herself, she had taken this legal windfall as a godsend and was quite content to accept her inheritance. After all, she rationalized, he was technically not related to her mother. And without a blood relationship, that was that as far as the Japanese inheritance laws were concerned.

Hiroshi decided to just walk away and get on with his life. He was also just a little relieved that he need not deal with all the estate paperwork with his first overseas business trip looming. Still it hurt that his sister could be so cool, almost cold, about things; but he was not the fighting type. And so in mid-August, he did just walk away. It would be November before Hiroshi learned the rest of the story.

*   *   *

SOON AFTER THE September tea party, word spread through the neighborhood that the reason Mrs. Ando's daughter had taken over the store was because Hiroshi was not Mrs. Ando's real son at all. Thus, he had no right to a share of the estate. This came as quite a surprise to the ladies—not just that mother and son were not related but that the inheritance law was filled with so many complicated twists and turns.

Mrs. Tanaka asked Jennifer if Shota could give them a simplified lecture on the workings of the inheritance system at one of their future meetings. The ladies all agreed that until one came face-to-face with it in their own lives, the inheritance system really was a vast unknown labyrinth full of spooky and unforeseen complexities. Jennifer said she would ask him, and that was the end of the story as far as the neighborhood ladies were concerned or so they thought.

It was an unseasonably warm September. In early October, one of Yumi Ando's neighbors began complaining of foul odors coming from the property. A complaint was filed, and the police were called in to investigate.

By the late October tea party, the whole neighborhood had finally learned of the Ando pet store saga; and the ladies discussed the details as they ate orange *manju*, bean paste-filled treats shaped to look just like miniature Halloween pumpkins.

The police discovered the shed was full of endangered animals, many of them now deceased. Mrs. Ando had been seen going in and out of the shed regularly before she died at the end of July; but no one had been observed going anywhere near the shed since then.

Further investigation revealed that some reptiles and other endangered creatures had died, but intervention had saved quite a few snakes, lizards and several rare tortoises. Without food, some reptiles could live two months or more and tortoises could last a year or two. Shota always found it amazing that tortoises had been crawling about at their own pace on this planet since the days of the dinosaurs.

The stench from the dead animals was almost overpowering. The local police quickly closed the door again and immediately called for backup from the district police station. And glimpsing the tip of a snake tail, it was suggested to headquarters that they also call in the famed Japan Snake Center in Gunma Prefecture for help with this case.

As the details of Mr. Ando's under-the-counter trade in endangered species were uncovered, Yumi was both shocked and appalled. Yumi Ando hadn't a clue as to what her father had been up to. She and her brother were never required to help out much in the shop, which offered just a few puppies and kittens, parakeets and goldfish. The store mainly dealt with pet food, pet accessories, grooming supplies—and endangered species.

Yumi vowed to cooperate with the police and turned over Mr. Ando's old cell phone which included the names of several suspected smugglers he had dealt with. They were pulled in for questioning, and she hoped her cooperation would result in their arrest.

Shota was not quite as optimistic. He didn't think they would get any jail time or even be prosecuted for that matter. Unless the police could find a clear paper trail of their smuggling routes and concrete evidence, it would be tough to prosecute and even harder to convict.

It was true endangered species could only legally be brought into Japan with the properly approved government paperwork. Yet once an animal was living in Japan, how could one prove it hadn't been born and bred right here?

Mr. Ando, of course, had kept no records on where the animals came from or how they got to him. Thus, the clueless Yumi Ando was quite safe from prosecution herself, but her tax problems were intensifying rapidly.

First, there was the matter of the inheritance tax on the property she had inherited. It turned out that land prices had risen a bit in their area, and the estate was valued at 50 million yen for inheritance tax purposes.

Under the standard inheritance tax rules, the first 30 million yen as well as six million yen per inheritor were exempt from taxation. This meant 36 million yen was tax-free, but she still owed tax on the remaining 14 million yen. And on any sum above 10 million yen and up to 30 million yen, the tax rate was 15 percent. So Yumi owed the Japanese government 1.5 million yen in inheritance tax.

Ironically, if she had shared with Hiroshi, they would have been able to deduct another six million yen. Then, they would have owed the government tax on only eight million yen, which was taxed at 10 percent. So, in effect, they would have owed the government just 800,000 yen. They would have halved their tax bill by sharing the estate.

However, this was all irrelevant now as the national tax authorities began poking around in the case. They discovered that for years Mr. Ando's business had not been reporting or paying any taxes at all on the considerable sums of money he had been making from his surreptitious, very lucrative, under-the-counter endangered species trade.

Mrs. Ando had technically inherited the business and his outstanding liabilities too. And since Yumi had now inherited all Mrs. Ando's assets and debts, it was all a big mess that it took an accountant considerable time to figure out.

What with legal and accounting fees, unpaid income taxes and penalties, and inheritance tax, Yumi faced a huge pile of bills. She was forced to sell the Ando property quickly at a great loss to avoid accruing even more tax penalties.

When Hiroshi returned to Japan in late November, he was astonished to discover his father's secret business and all that had happened in the two months he was gone.

Realizing he had narrowly avoided being caught in the middle of all this, he felt sorry for his sister and offered to help her resettle. Family, Yumi now realized, was everything.

In the end, Yumi just barely had enough money left to place a down payment on a tiny, two-room condo on the other side of Tokyo where no one knew her or her story.

At the ladies' December *bonenkai* (year-forgetting party), as the women nibbled on a batch of Jennifer's homemade Christmas cookies, Mrs. Higashi reported that bulldozers had arrived to tear down the Ando house and shed. The structures were to be replaced by a five-story, curb-hugging apartment building—another sort of blight on the leafy suburban neighborhood.

THE TAPIOCA SISTERS

ONE FROSTY WINTER afternoon, the neighborhood ladies were again gathered at Mrs. Kawasaki's house. They were enjoying *o-shiruko*, a sweet, red bean soup served with a small, chewy *mochi* rice cake in the middle. It was the perfect, warming treat for such a bitterly cold day. While they ate, the ladies learned of another fascinating case. It was one of those simple, unfortunate mishaps that humans can get themselves into if they let down their defenses even for a moment.

At the previous gathering, Mrs. Nishi had announced she and her husband were invited on a ten-day, all-expenses paid *onsen* tour by her childhood best friend. The couples would travel south by train and stay in hot spring inns each night as they soaked their way across the archipelago. The tour was to end at the famed Yufuin spa near Beppu on the southern island of Kyushu. It was to be the dream trip of a lifetime for them. The only problem was that Mrs. Nishi didn't know what to do with her miniature schnauzer, Elvis, while she was gone. She inquired whether any of the ladies knew of a good dog hotel in the area.

Mrs. Higashi suggested a place on the far side of town where Vick had once stayed—with once being the operative word. She admitted that being a beagle, he was not about to take that kind of treatment without a protest. He howled and howled until he had every dog and cat in the place in a frenzy for the night. The owner banned him from ever coming back again, but Mrs. Higashi had thought it would be fine for a quiet dog like Elvis.

As the ladies sipped their *o-shiruko* on this cold afternoon, someone casually inquired when Mrs. Nishi was leaving on her trip.

"We are not going after all," she replied, her voice tinged with sadness and regret.

"What? You were so looking forward to it."

Indeed, Mrs. Nishi had been talking about nothing else for weeks.

"What happened?" Jennifer asked.

Mrs. Nishi was a little hesitant to explain at first. It was not her story to tell. But since no one in the neighborhood knew her childhood friend who lived on the other side of Tokyo, she decided she could explain in detail.

"My friend Haruko, who planned the trip, came into an inheritance, quite a large inheritance. She had used most of it to pay off her mortgage and help with the educational needs of her grandchildren. Still, she had enough left for this one grand vacation. Then something came up. She suddenly had to use the money for that, and now we can't go."

"How dreadful! What happened?"

What ensued was the very instructive tale of *The Tapioca Sisters,* three sisters who made a very surprising discovery.

Haruko was the eldest. Their father had named each of them after the season in which they were born. So there was Haruko born in April, Natsuko born in July and Akiko born in October. He chose those simple, practical, seasonal names for them as he was a practical, straightforward fellow. However, he was fastidious about the paperwork of life.

Their mother had died while Haruko was still in high school, and she had looked after her two younger sisters almost as a mother would. All three women were very close and devoted to each other. They seldom argued and were never jealous of each other. They each knew their place and role in the family, and they carried them out.

Haruko was their leader and advisor. Natsuko, the middle child, was the peacemaker in the family. The youngest daughter, Akiko, was the one chosen for higher education. She was given a chance to attend college and make a career for herself. Feeling they had been forced to marry quite young, her two elder sisters wanted Akiko to have the opportunities their generation had missed.

While Akiko had her career, somewhere along the way she missed her chance to marry. She was the only one not married when their father, who had been in declining health for several years, took ill.

Being a practical man, he had decided to put all his financial affairs in order before he passed on. He realized the estate could become complicated because he owned a rather ramshackle house that sat on a very lucrative, little piece of Tokyo real estate. He decided to sell the property himself while he was still alive and could negotiate a fair price for it. This would save his daughters from having to rush to sell the property to pay the inheritance tax bill, which would be hefty and come due ten months after his death.

Then, their father set himself up in a little retirement facility for his last year or two of life. He thought this plan would turn his only asset into more useful cash and also make things easier for his daughters. They would only need to visit or shop for him occasionally rather than be exhausted by his care.

Still, the three sisters, who were very close all their lives, took turns visiting and caring for him. On Mondays and Wednesdays, Haruko went to see him. On Tuesdays and Thursdays, Natsuko sat with him. Akiko went on Saturdays and Sundays. On Friday evenings, all three sisters got together to relax, compare notes and dine in one of Tokyo's many tapioca cafes. Quite the rage in the capital in recent years, all three women loved exploring them and discovering the many innovative and artistic ways tapioca could be prepared.

The sisters all had such a passion for tapioca that once Akiko, who had studied Japanese literature in translation at college, nicknamed them *The Tapioca Sisters*. This was a pun on *The Makioka Sisters,* the title of the English translation of *Sasameyuki,* the famed Junichiro Tanizaki novel about a family of four sisters.

When their father died, the Tapioca Sisters, who were very close and trusted each other completely, did not fight over their inheritance. Since their father had made sure it was just this nice, large lump of cash sitting in the bank, it was very easy to divide. Since the sisters got along so well, they merely split the money into three equal portions and signed the *isan bunkatsu kyogisho* agreement that settled the estate. This made things very simple.

The rather disinterested accountant just reminded them each to pay their share of the inheritance tax as soon as possible, and the paperwork was finished. Haruko and Natsuko paid up immediately and rejoiced that things had been settled so very quickly and simply, or so they thought.

"Oh, oh," Jennifer muttered. She seemed to know what was coming next.

Mrs. Tanaka did too, as she asked: "You mean, they didn't pay all the inheritance tax to the government first before they divided the money between themselves and signed the final paperwork?"

"No," said Mrs. Nishi. "They didn't."

"Oh, don't tell me they got a horrendous surprise later," Mrs. Tanaka inquired.

"Yes, they did."

Mrs. Higashi was not sure what they were talking about so Jennifer threw in Shota's legal opinion.

"Oh yes, Shota always says you do have to be careful with that since Japan has joint payment responsibility. It's called *rentai noufu gimu*, isn't it?"

Mrs. Higashi had never heard of this before so Mrs. Tanaka explained: "If each inheritor is left to pay their own share of the overall tax bill on their own, then all the inheritors are still at risk until all of the tax is paid. It means they all have a joint responsibility to see the government gets its share. They are all still liable for the tax until it is paid. If one inheritor can't pay, then the only option the other inheritors have is to try to persuade the delinquent inheritor to work out a repayment plan with the government. If that's not possible, then the other heirs have to come up with the money themselves. And all this time, interest is being charged and accumulating on the unpaid amount."

Mrs. Nishi noted this is what had happened to the Tapioca Sisters. All the ladies gasped as she continued with her story.

Akiko was a rather lonely woman. As her father's condition worsened, she sought companionship and someone to talk to. She met a man from Kyoto online who seemed nice and understanding and cultured. They communicated while she went through the difficult period of her father's decline. After his death, her online friend was considerate, consoling and supportive. He soon invited her to Kyoto where he wined and dined her, made her feel special and even gave her an expensive brand bag. How could she imagine he was not serious and reliable?

A week or two later, he called to say he was having some difficulties with his business. He hated to ask, but could she possibly transfer some money, quite a large sum of money, to his account to help him out of this rough spot?

After she did so, he called immediately to thank her. He then said he had to attend an out-of-town business meeting over the weekend, but he would call her again on Monday just as soon as he returned. But, of course, he never did. The phone number and email address also disappeared, and the brand bag, like him, turned out to be a fake.

Then Akiko remembered that he had never taken her to his home or office in Kyoto. They had dined in restaurants, or ate lunches in the park, or strolled through temple gardens.

Akiko thought of reporting him to the police, but deep down she still had feelings for him. Besides, she had to admit that he had not actually promised her anything. He simply asked for money, and she had sent it. Where was the crime in that? He had never promised to marry her, or even pay her back for that matter. She had simply been stupid, and she didn't want the embarrassment of her dear sisters finding out how foolish and silly she had been.

Akiko was beside herself, but she also had to admit it was a common enough scam and a hard-learned life lesson. She had used a large portion of her inheritance money to pay off her condo mortgage first, so she did have a secure place to live. She was still working so she would get through this although her retirement years might be considerably harsher because of this miscalculation. Yet, she consoled herself with the realization that she was still healthy, employed, with no loans hanging over her head, and no dependents to worry about. She would be eligible for a pension in a few more years. She had it better than most. She was determined to just put this unfortunate incident behind her and not let on to her sisters that anything had happened. She was glad she hadn't told them about her foolish romance. What a mess, she told herself, but at least my sisters won't have to know. That was where she was mistaken.

In all the excitement, she had completely forgotten she owed almost three million yen in inheritance tax. When the inheritance tax deadline passed and she hadn't paid up, all three sisters were eventually informed. Akiko had to reveal her situation and explain she had no idea how she could raise the money. It would be all she could do to survive on her small pension in a few years. With interest penalties accruing, the sisters had to come up with a plan as soon as possible. So Haruko and Natsuko, who always considered the three of them a team, each chipped in half the money and paid off Akiko's tax bill.

That devoured the last of Haruko's inheritance. The *onsen* vacation was no longer a viable dream. Meanwhile, Natsuko would have to give her grandchildren a little less than she planned. Yet the sisters agreed they would get through this together as a family, as they always got through everything.

Mrs. Kawasaki thought about the poor Akiko and just how much there was to deal with in life. "People can't even grow old without keeping their wits about them constantly," she sighed.

Bunta agreed. He was happy with his new feline life and none of that tedious human stuff to worry about anymore. Sitting in Mrs. Kawasaki's lap, he purred happily and the ladies all smiled at such a contented cat.

When Jennifer related the story of the Tapioca Sisters to Shota that evening, he was not at all sympathetic.

"If this Akiko wanted a true and loyal friend, she should have got a dog. You won't find a more devoted, reliable companion anywhere," he sniffed and, of course, he was right.

ACKNOWLEDGEMENTS

FOREST RIVER PRESS began with a rash idea in 2003: "If no publisher wants to publish my first book *The Couch Potato's Guide to Japan: Inside the World of Japanese TV*, I'll just have to do it myself." Self-publishing was a rash, overly naive and harebrained scheme back then before digital publishing arrived.

Now, many books later, Forest River Press miraculously survives and turns 20 in 2023. It is still a kid at heart though—still learning, experimenting, making mistakes and trying to correct them, not earning much, and yet stubbornly resisting doing what it doesn't want to do. In the case of FRP, that means bypassing social media and dynamic marketing techniques. Yet somehow, it still carries on, and that's all any of us can do.

Self-publishing can be a lonely pursuit, and it is important to look to the knowledge and advice of others as one forges ahead. Many people—friends, you dear readers, and even a few kind strangers—have helped me stay on track over the years and make my publishing dreams a reality. Forest River Press books are a product of all that good will and assistance.

For this book, I would especially like to thank my family for their patience, encouragement and support—my lifelong mentor, Grace Lang, my husband Jun and especially my daughter Julie, who creates the artwork and cover designs for all the Forest River Press books.

As always, I owe a great debt of gratitude to Beth Sakanishi, a fellow writer and friend of almost four decades, who has tirelessly read all my many drafts and has offered wise comments, prompt advice and constant feedback on this and all my writing projects. I am also very grateful to my dear writing friends Sally Kobayashi, Margaret Shibuya, Karen Hill Anton and Lynne Riggs for their help, advice, encouragement and interest.

Special thanks also to Paul Salvette of BBeBooks in Bangkok, who does a great job on the e-book conversions and interior layouts for the paperback versions of all my books.

Without the help and support of all these people, my publishing dreams would have faded away long ago. I could not have done it without you all. Thank you!

ABOUT THE AUTHOR

WM. (WILHELMINA) PENN was born and raised in Pittsburgh, Pa. and has lived in Japan since 1973. That was so long ago that when her flight from Europe to Tokyo stopped to refuel in Iran, the pilot let everyone out to stretch their legs on the Tehran tarmac.

In the five decades since, she has been a student, teacher, writer, part-time pumpkin farmer, occasional translator, and a weekly columnist for the English-language editions of both the *Yomiuri* (25 years from 1987-2012) and *Asahi* (13 years from 1991-2004) newspapers. Nordic walking and Korean TV dramas are her current passions. She can be contacted via her website www.forestriverpress.com.

FOREST RIVER PRESS
**—BOOKS AS REFRESHING AS
A WALK IN THE WOODS—**

Made in the USA
Middletown, DE
08 November 2022

14377735R00097